WHAT IS IRIDOLOGY?
ILLUSTRATED

Iridology is the science and practice of analyzing the iris, the most complex tissue structure in the human anatomy. Iridology reveals the presence of tissue inflammation in the body, where it is located and what stage it has reached—acute, subacute, chronic or degenerative. The iris reveals the level of constitutional strength, inherent weaknesses, state of health and the transitions that take place in a person's organs and tissues according to the way he lives.

by

BERNARD JENSEN

ALL RIGHTS RESERVED. No part of this publication may be reproduced, stored in a retrieval system or transmitted in any form or by any means: electronic, mechanical, photocopying, recording or otherwise, without prior written permission from the author/publisher.
This book is intended for use as an information source. It is not intended as advice for self diagnosis or a prescription for self treatment. It is hoped that the information contained herein will stimulate thought and encourage the adoption of a beneficial lifestyle.

Second Edition

Copyright 1984 Bernard Jensen
ALL RIGHTS RESERVED

Published by Bernard Jensen, 24360 Old Wagon Road, Escondido, California 92027; Phone: 619-749-2727, FAX 619-740-1248.

ISBN #0-932615-22-8

WHAT IS IRIDOLOGY?

Iridology is the science and practice of analyzing the iris, the most complex tissue structure in the human anatomy. Iridology reveals the presence of tissue inflammation in the body, where it is located and what stage it has reached—acute, subacute, chronic or degenerative. The iris reveals the level of constitutional strength, inherent weaknesses, state of health and the transitions that take place in a person's organs and tissues according to the way he lives.

Under magnification, the iris, the color part of the eye, appears as a magnificent landscape, a world of minute detail in which thousands of fine white fibers are organized into three tiers or layers of vascular arcades. According to one physiology text, 28,000 individual nerve fibers connect with every cell and chromatophore in the iris stroma, the main body of the iris. Under the stroma are two separate, slightly overlapping muscle groups, one to dilate the pupil, the other to contract it. These muscles, the dilator muscle and the sphincter muscle, are the only ones in the body derived from nerve tissue in the developing embryo, and they are richly endowed with nerves—about one nerve for every 5-to-10 muscle cells as compared to one nerve for every 200-300 muscle cells elsewhere in the body. Surrounding the sphincter muscle which controls pupil contraction is a frill called the autonomic nerve wreath by iridologists. Nerve control of the area inside the autonomic wreath is parasympathetic, while the sympathetic nerves control the area of the iris outside the wreath. The iris, therefore, contains a communication system capable of handling a great deal of information, since the sympathetic and parasympathetic systems, together, control every organ in the body and keep the brain constantly informed concerning the metabolic status of each one.

The eyes are extensions of the brain, and through them 86% of our learning takes place. But we also notice that the eyes do far more than transmit information to the visual cortex of the brain. When we are excited or emotionally aroused, our pupils dilate; when we are disgusted or tense, the pupils contract. From this, we know that the nerves to the sphincter and dilator muscles are connected with the limbic system, the emotional brain. Certain drugs such as alcohol, atropine and opiates also cause pupillary changes, so we know the iris nerves respond to chemical changes in the body. Walter Lang, A German researcher, points out that nerve impulses from the hypothalamus and thalamus, which monitor tissue conditions all over the body, may reach the irides via the oculomotor nucleus and the Edinger-Westphal nucleus. We find there is an adequate scientific basis to explain how it is possible for iris changes to be reflexly correlated with tissue changes elsewhere in the body. Perhaps the poet was expressing more than he knew when he wrote, "The eye is the window to the soul."

Each iris is unique, although the pattern of neural information brought to it is identical in each person. We can visualize iris topology in terms of geography, mapped out into specific territories which represent specific portions of the anatomy. Each of these "territories" represents the current health status of a specific gland, organ or tissue structure in the body, as monitored by the brain and reflexly displayed in the iris by a continuously operating network of neural impulses. Over the past century and more, iridologists have painstakingly mapped the iris by carefully correlating known health problems in certain parts of the body with observed structural landmarks and changes in the irides. The stomach, they found, is always represented by a circular ring surrounding the pupil, while the bowel is represented by the remaining portion of the iris between the stomach area and the autonomic nerve wreath. The brain is reflexly represented by the top part of the iris, while the leg and foot are at the bottom. We will see this in more precise detail when we come to my iridology chart.

To establish a more or less universal framework for locating reflex features of the iris, I have used the hour positions of the standard clock, 1 to 12 o'clock, with 10 subdivisions between each hour position. Thus, we say the lungs are at 3 o'clock in the left iris and 9 o'clock in the right iris.

The brain is represented from 11 to 1 o'clock in both irides, and the leg and foot at 6 o'clock in both. The right side of the body is represented in the right iris, the left side in the left iris. Some parts of the anatomy, such as the stomach, bowel and brain are found in both irides, while others are specific to one iris. The spleen, for example, on the left side of the body, reflexes only to the left iris, while the liver, on the right side of the body, reflexes only to the right iris. The iridologist interprets the various shapes, patterns and configurations in and around the countless numbers of iris fibers to understand what is going on in the body.

Presently, as in the past, primary health care doctors have used this form of analysis along with other diagnostic techniques to develop a more complete profile of patients' health care needs. Iris analysis offers information that is simply unavailable through conventional laboratory tests and interpretations of a patient's aches, pains and other symptoms. These may signal that something is wrong, but they seldom reveal where the source of the problem is in the body or which organs are affected. Iridology does this effectively, efficiently and reliably without requiring tissue biopsies, exploratory surgery, injections of dyes or chemicals to make some organ appear distinct on X-rays or other dangerous, painful and expensive diagnostic aids. Iridology is safe, painless and non-invasive to the body.

The eyes have long been used to aid in diagnosis, the most obvious example being the fundus examination. As Louis H. Schwartz, MD, has written, "The signs of constitutional disease frequently appear in the eye before they show up elsewhere in the body, or they may be present only in the eye." He is referring to symptoms of multiple sclerosis, coronary heart disease, atherosclerosis, kidney disease and others familiar to ophthalmologists who peer into our inner eyes through the ophthalmoscope. Iridology simply extends this concept of reflex symptomatology to the iris.

At this point, we come to a very important distinction. Iridology does not diagnose disease. Iris analysis reveals abnormal tissue conditions, inflammation, toxic-laden organs and tissues—but it does not diagnose disease. These states are the fundamental precursors of any disease, but we find that similar patterns of tissue pathology in different individuals, as shown by iridology, result in different eventual disease outcomes. One person may develop arthritis, another eczema and still another, ovarian cysts, from the same basic causes. Disease follows the route of least resistance in the body, attacking the weakest body systems and tissues first. Because these weaknesses vary so much from person to person, the particular form of disease manifestation can't be reliably predicted in the individual. Moreover, disease, by definition consists of categorizing certain groups of symptoms under particular names. Not until those symptoms come out in full bloom can an individual be diagnosed as having a particular disease—such as cancer, tuberculosis, psoriasis or asthma. Iridology doesn't see symptoms. It sees tissue conditions, and it often sees them long before any symptoms appear.

The American Cancer Society says it takes as long as 20 years to develop some types of cancer. All chronic diseases take time to develop before they manifest in pain, fever, heart palpitations, lumps, discharges and other symptoms. During this developmental state while symptoms are nonexistent—the preclinical stage—tissue damage in the body is slowly, gradually, cumulatively taking place. The greatest advantage of iridology is its ability to identify the presence of early tissue pathology in the preclinical stage. Iridology can assist the doctor in "nipping a disease in the bud," so to speak.

"An ounce of prevention is worth a pound of cure," so the saying goes. The great strength of iridology lies in its value as a preventive tool, a form of analysis which identifies problems in the body in time for relatively simple and inexpensive forms of correction such as diet changes, exercise and dealing with sources of stress on the job, in the home, in the lifestyle of the individual.

Today, iridologists are beginning to understand that the full potential of iridology is much greater than assumed in past years. The total quantity of information in the iris is almost unbelievable, yet we have managed to translate only a relatively small portion of this "body language." A closer look at the iris with the aid of space-age technology will show, I believe, that the iris fibers present such accurate microcomputer readouts of body functions and conditions that individual health programs can be designed to avoid chronic disease and maximize the experienced well-being of each person, as well as to assist those with existing diseases to reverse and eliminate the causes of their symptoms.

It is also abundantly evident that iridology could be an invaluable aid to Western medicine by providing a more wholistic context for the understanding and treatment of disease, and by demonstrating the value of correct nutrition in the restoration of tissue damaged in the course of disease.

I have spent over 50 years in sanitarium work, watching many patients getting well and others not progressing as they should. From the beginning, I yearned for some non-invasive way of checking what was going on in a patient's body without having to subject it to radiation, cut into it or introduce some other painful test procedure. When I encountered iridology, I found the answer.

The iris is an excellent barometer of the "health weather conditions" in the body. Changes in the structure of the iris reflexly correspond to changes in body tissue in observable ways over a period of time. When we have good health, it is to some extent evident in skin color and tone, in the luster and body of the hair, in the way a person moves and holds his body; but the eye, as an extension of the brain, is the most sensitive reflex organ available for examination. We can tell a few things from the skin, but the information-density in the iris is so much greater that it is easily the optimum choice for examination.

One of the most difficult aspects of iridology for me was that I had to give up the idea of diagnosing disease. Diseases, after all, were a well-established and convenient means of putting health problems into individual boxes or packages. But I noticed that most diseases were defined in terms of symptoms, and the peculiar thing about symptoms is that they seldom give a doctor enough information to get at the basic cause of the problem. Nor is the disease necessarily cured when the symptoms are made to disappear by some ingenious therapy or miracle drug. Iridology taught me that the basic conditions which so often later give rise to disease are either nutrient deficiencies or toxic accumulations in specific parts of the body. By taking care of these basic causes, I found that a much larger percentage of my patients was getting well. This, I believe, is the correct basis for all successful treatment. There is a place for drugs, a place for surgery, a place for osteopathy, a place for chiropractic, a place for homeopathy in the healing arts. Nearly all healing arts have developed because they had a certain degree of success with cases that did not respond to other existing therapies. But, unless toxins are eliminated from the body, and unless proper nutrients are provided in the necessary quantities, tissue repair cannot take place. This is the "bottom line," as they say.

I was given an award at an international gathering of doctors in San Remo, Italy, about 15 years ago. Speaker after speaker talked about diagnosing and treating specific diseases in specific organs and tissues of the body. One speaker discussed scraping a tooth to deal with the infection at its root. When my turn came, I brought out the fact that the rest of that patient's body was attached to that tooth. In other words, 90% or more of the body is connected to any infected, inflamed or diseased tooth, kidney or shoulder joint. Yet, without good digestion, we cannot have good assimilation or good bowel activity. Without good bowel activity, we cannot get rid of toxic materials in the body. And, how can we repair and rebuild tissue with toxic material working in the bloodstream? We must start with a clean body to activate the healing process.

This is the premise I have worked on. I cleaned up the bloodstream, introduced patients to a good basic diet and encouraged changes in those areas of their lifestyles that were contributing to health problems. I tried to teach patients that they have to "clean up their act," so to speak. Many of them had tried everything else, but this was an alternative way, a way of taking care of conditions and ailments that were not responding well to other therapies. And, it worked. It still works.

I have never attempted to take care of any disease. Instead, I take care of the human being on the other end of the disease, and the disease leaves. That's the way of prevention. If I catch a patient in time, there is no disease to treat. If doctors did more educating, they wouldn't have to do so much medicating.

We find that the body molds or adapts to whatever environment we put it in, as well as it can. The body is a servant to the mind; it has no innate intelligence of its own. If we feed it junk food, polluted water and drugs, it will adapt to them as well as it can. If we give it cigarettes and polluted air to breathe, it will adapt as well as it can. If we subject it to high stress on the job, misery in our homelife and bitter, angry attitudes toward others, it will adapt. Sometimes this adaptation process builds cancer, heart disease, hypoglycemia or ulcers, and at that point, an intelligent person might realize that he or she has been expecting the body to adapt to an environment unfit for survival.

But, who made the choices that brought on the disease?
Our bodies need to be led. They need a right way to go.
How can we tell if we are leading the body the right way?

That's the question that led me to the study of iridology. I needed a type of analysis that would show me whether a particular health program, a particular nutritional regimen, was working for my patients. I didn't want to wait for symptoms. I wanted to make tissue changes during the "preclinical stage," and I wanted some means of checking myself, some means of monitoring progress. Iridology gave me a form of analysis that worked beautifully with nutrition and other natural approaches to healing, such as exercise, fresh air, herbs and so on.

HERING'S LAW OF CURE

While studying homeopathy, I found what we might call a "sleeper," an obscure law of healing developed by Constantine Hering, a 19th century European homeopathic physician. Hering's law of cure states,"All cure comes from within out, from the head down and in reverse order as the symptoms first appeared." This somewhat peculiar law, I found, applies with surprising accuracy to the natural healing of chronic diseases (which represent about 80% of all cases treated by doctors in the U.S.). It refers to the reversal of the course of disease and to the healing crisis, the natural means the body uses to get rid of substances harmful to its tissues prior to the restoration of those tissues.

As I considered Hering's law of cure in relation to iridology, I knew that healing lines were an indication of the reversal of disease processes. The white fibers always seemed to come into the deepest level of any lesion or lacuna first, working their way "within out." The brain, referred to as "the head" in Hering's law, is the key to the healing process because control of both the endocrine system and the autonomic nerves, crucial in triggering reversal of disease, are there. By cleansing the bloodstream, brain function is elevated and made more efficient in directing physiological response to damaged tissue. In this sense, "all cure" comes "from the head down." We also notice that there is a psychosomatic component to all disease states, and we can assist the patient in releasing psychological hindrances and in taking a positive, assertive stance toward healing—which speeds it up. Finally, as the whole body grows stronger, the patient encounters a sudden healing crisis in which old symptoms return and toxins are discharged, in preparation for tissue repair. The most recent symptoms are experienced first. Subsequent healing crises may bring back symptoms that reach further back in time, even to a person's childhood, "in reverse order as symptoms first appeared." As hypoactive tissue is elevated in metabolic function, the autonomic nerves to that tissue signal the brain, and the brain transmits this information to the irides.

In short, when we see iris lesions filling with white healing filaments, we are observing reflex indications of tissue repair in the body—the reversal of disease. I believe every disease is associated with one or more nutritional deficiencies. By adding the proper nutritional balance to a person's diet, we can make a change in his condition. Again, the body molds to what we put into it, and correct diet exercises a powerful restoring influence as long-term deficiencies are taken care of. Tissue in the iris stroma changes to reflect tissue healing in the body, as we see the evidence in the iris.

There are over 3,000 doctors in Germany using iridology today. It is being used in France, Russia, China, Australia, Latin America and South Africa. I believe this is just the beginning.

IRIS SIGNS

There are many reflex indications in the iris that iridologists have learned to interpret, but we must realize that none of them indicates pathology in the eye itself. Iris signs are only indications of compromised tissue integrity elsewhere in the body, with the exception of the five-sense area near 12 o'clock, which can show, reflexly, damage to the eye itself. This, of course, should be self evident.

Constitutional Strength. We discuss this in more depth elsewhere. Briefly, a fine, closely-woven fiber structure indicates a strong natural immune system, a body resistant to disease with rapid recuperative powers.

Inherent Weaknesses. These are gaps in iris fibers, indicating organs, glands or tissues in the body which are metabolically weaker than others. They absorb nutrients more slowly and get rid of wastes less efficiently than other tissues.

Lesions, Lacunae, Crypts. These are terms usually applied to inherent weaknesses manifesting acute (white), subacute (gray), chronic (dark gray) or degenerative (black) indications.

Psora or Drug Settlements. Black, red, brown, orange or yellow flecks, streaks or patches indicate drug or chemical settlements, inherited or acquired. We cannot distinguish individual drugs—there are simply too many with related chemical structures—but we can sometimes see iron, iodine or sulfur. These may indicate actual or potential problems in the tissues where they are settled. A murky iris is often associated with a history of excessive use of many drugs. These drug areas may become lighter, but they do not leave entirely.

Acidity. When the iris fibers are white and raised throughout the iris, an overacidic condition in the body is recognized. This is irritating to all tissues.

Nerve Rings. Curved furrows following the curvature of the iris circumference may be found in the form of arcs of varying lengths. These indicate the state of stress the person is under. The iridologist looks at the beginning and end of nerve rings to see which organs are under stress.

Lymphatic Rosary. Small, whitish or yellowish "beads" which appear to be strung just inside part or all of the iris circumference indicate lymphatic congestion. They look like small cotton balls.

Scurf Rim. A dark ring around part or all of the external rim of the iris indicates an underactive skin which is not eliminating as it should.

Cholesterol/Calcium Ring. A translucent-to-opaque ring just inside the outer rim of the iris, appearing to be a deposit in the cornea, indicates hardening of the arteries.

Anemia in the Extremities. A hazy, semi-opaque ring inside the iris perimeter, in the corneal layer, shows poor circulation, inadequate iron or a low red blood cell count.

Arcus Senilis. A white, yellow or bluish-white crescent arc, which appears to be scleral tissue "capping" the cornea, is a sign of cerebral anemia.

Radii Solaris. Appearing like spokes in a wheel, these iris signs, originating in the bowel area and radiating outward, generally indicate toxic material from the bowel being transmitted via the bloodstream, to the tissues or organs at the outer edge of the spokes.

Prolapsus. A flattening or dip at the top of the autonomic wreath indicates prolapsus of the transverse colon, usually with resulting pressure on the pelvic organs. This has been repeatedly verified by X-rays.

Diverticula. Small lesions radiating out from the autonomic wreath indicate diverticula or bowel pockets, which are sometimes impacted with fecal material. They can be a source of low-grade infection and may allow toxic material to pass through the bowel wall.

Interpreting these signs properly takes training and practice, and it is well to realize what we cannot read in the iris.

THE IRIS DOES NOT REVEAL

1. Diseases
2. Pregnancy
3. Gallstones or kidney stones
4. Surgical operations
5. Length of life
6. Psychic readings

No iris analysis by a novice should be taken seriously. There some who have used iridology incorrectly, and I suggest caution in approaching the subject, to avoid misunderstanding and misinterpretation. In the hands of an expert, however, it can be a wonderful tool.

A DISCOVERY IN 1853

The little fellow—the owl picture on the following page—is like the one who started modern iridology by getting himself caught in a trap in a Hungarian boy's garden. The leg sign in the lower part of the eye is only one of the 90 areas we have identified in the human iris since Ignatz von Peczely's time.

Dr. von Peczely's first iridology chart is also shown with the owl picture. You will see there are no exact lines where the lungs begin and end, because his knowledge was probably not that precise. Some of the glands are shown, as are the back, arm and leg areas. There is not much in the brain area. Like most basic discoveries, only a few crude aspects of this art were found out in the beginning. But it was enough to inspire others to carry on the investigation.

The earliest efforts to correlate changes in the iris with changes in health are said to date back to the Chaldeans. Theodore Kriege, a prominent German iridologist, reported that the first documented reference to iris analysis had been traced to the 17th century physician, Philippus Meyens, who described reflexive signs in the iris in his book *Chiromatica Medica*, published in Dresden.

By 1695, references to iridology could be found in the works of Johann Eltzholtz; and, in 1786, almost a century later, Christian Haertels published a dissertation in Gottingen titled *De Oculo et Signo*, (The eye and its signs.)

The father of iridology as it is known today, however, was Dr. Ignatz von Peczely (1826-1911), a Hungarian physician. Von Peczely's discovery of iridology, according to tradition, was almost pure coincidence, as we have mentioned.

Von Peczely became interested in homeopathy after his university graduation, and began treating those who came to him for advice. History records that he saved his own mother's life with homeopathic remedies. While treating patients, he recalled the incident with the owl in his garden, and began looking for correlations between his patient's ailments and the appearance of their irides. When a local physician formally complained of this "quackery," von Peczely was hauled into court.

In self defense, the young Hungarian analyzed his accuser's eyes and accurately described several past ailments for which the physician had been treated. Dumbfounded, the doctor dropped his fraud charges.

Possibly because of this event, von Peczely began the study of medicine at the age of 36, receiving his doctorate at the medical college in Vienna, Austria. His internship provided many opportunities to study the irides of hospital patients before and after surgery, and to perform autopsies to confirm the existence of ailments he had diagnosed from the eyes of people before they died.

Opening a homeopathic practice in Budapest in 1869, Dr. von Peczely soon developed a large clientele of patients. In 1880, he published a book titled, ***Discoveries in the Realms of***

A DISCOVERY IN 1853

- IRIS CHART -
Ignatz Von Peczely

In the early 1800s, Ignatz von Peczely of Hungary, caught an owl in his garden. In the struggle, he accidentally broke the bird's leg. He observed a black stripe rising in the owl's eye. He nursed the owl back to health and released the bird, but it remained in the garden. Von Peczely observed white and crooked lines in the eye where the stripe had been and eventually they became just a tiny black spot surrounded by white lines and shading. Von Peczely became a physician and never forgot the incident with the owl. That is how iridology began.

Nature and the Art of Healing. At first ignored, his work was later given a great deal of attention in Germany.

Strange as it may seem, an 8-year-old boy living in Stockholm Sweden, named Nils Liljequist, began studying eyes, while the 33-year-old von Peczely was carrying out his iris studies. Liljequist independently made many discoveries similar to those of von Peczely over the years, and published a book titled *Om Oegendiagnosen* in 1893. The book was translated into English in 1916.

Iridology caught on more in Germany and Austria than anywhere else, partly as a result of the influential work of an iridologist called Pastor Felke, who had many students. By the turn of the century, iridology had crossed the Atlantic to the United States.

Henry Edward Lane (or Lahn), MD, of Austria, may have been the first to bring iris analysis to the U.S. Lane's student, Dr. Henry Lindlahr, MD, spread the news of iridology through the magazine *Nature Cure*, then published a six-volume series of books on nature cure philosophy, which included a volume titled **Iridiagnosis and Other Diagnostic Methods** (1919).

From 1922-24, I worked with Dr. Lindlahr at his Nature Cure Sanitarium near Chicago, learning iridology and the proper handling of the healing crisis. In San Francisco, I continued my studies of iridology with Dr. R.M. McLain, a successful chiropractor and iridologist, for four years. I arranged for further study in 1929 with Dr. F.W. Collins, director of the Association of Iridology and translator of Peter Johannes Thiel's 1905 work, *The Diagnosis of Disease by Observation of the Eye*. Collins had also published a volume of his own work.

Later, my discussions with Dr. J. Haskel Kritzer, MD, and Dr. John Arnold, DC, did much to further my understanding of the applications and philosophy of iridology. Dr. Arnold was the founder of the World Iridology Fellowship, and Dr. Kritzer had written a textbook, *Iridiagnosis*, as well as developing one of the first iridology charts useful for instructing beginning students. It was Dr. Kritzer who urged me to consider teaching iridology as well as using it with patients.

My work with Dr. Collins included drawing 500 irides in color, showing the lesions and other iris signs, from patients. This is where I really learned iris analysis.

THE EYES HAVE IT

In nature, we find a wide variety of eyes in insect, reptile, amphibian, bird and animal life. The eyes are survival instruments, showing the presence of food and shelter, warning of danger, finding avenues of escape from pursuit. There are other sensory mechanisms in all living species, but the eyes are often the most important.

One species of moth shown on the following page has a design on its wings that appears exactly like a pair of staring eyes when the moth is at rest. Since few birds or animals will go after some creature that is staring right at them, the eye-wings serve as protection for this moth.

Frogs' eyes are surprisingly insensitive to color, texture and shade, but they are amazingly sensitive to movement. The movement of something small in front of its face will send the frog's sticky tongue darting out in search of dinner, while any large movement sends the frog plopping into the pond for shelter.

The honeybee has a compound hexagonal eye which organizes the landscape into hexagonal frames. It is no accident that the honeybee shapes its honeycomb into six-sided cylinders, because that is how it sees everything.

Nocturnal creatures such as owls, rats and others often have highly-sensitive retinas that give them better vision at night than other creatures.

The eye is truly a miraculous structure in most creatures; the dominant means for learning about and adapting to the environment.

CHART DEVELOPMENT

The purpose of the iridology chart is very simple. If you wanted to find a building on the corner of 42nd Street and Sunrise Avenue in a large city you had not visited before, you would need a map. The same problem exists for an iridologist in locating the kidney area or the pleura area in a patient's eye. The iridology chart is, basically, a map of the reflex areas of the iris showing the locations and outlines of the various parts of the human anatomy.

When I began my iridology work, there were several different iridology charts in use. I took the best of these charts, added features from other charts that I had verified from experience and included several discoveries of my own. Since my chart was published in the 1950s, it has come to be used in countries all over the world. When I lectured at the University of Canton on Mainland China, I was shown a copy of my iridology chart translated into Chinese.

At the top of our Chart Development sheet is the chart of Professor Peter Johannes Thiel (translated into Spanish), who taught Dr. F.W. Collins, one of my teachers. It was Dr. Collins who had me draw 500 irides to develop my skill in analysis. The relationship between Thiel's and Collins' charts is fairly clear, despite the symbolic picturing of actual anatomical parts in Thiel's work. Notice that the concept of concentric circular zones is well developed in Dr. Collins' chart.

Dr. Henry Lindlahr's chart, based on the charts of Lane and Nils Liljequist, is very detailed, but the boundaries or outlines of organ reflex areas are left for the student to refine on his own.

In my Chart to Iridology, the 12-clock positions are used for easy radial location of organs, with 10 subdivisions between each number. Zones are laid out to assist with depth location and most organs and systems are outlined clearly. I have used the best ideas and data from other charts and from my own research, and have tried to design it for practical use.

There is about 80% agreement among iridologists on the organization of the iridology chart, but there is room for further research, refinement and discovery.

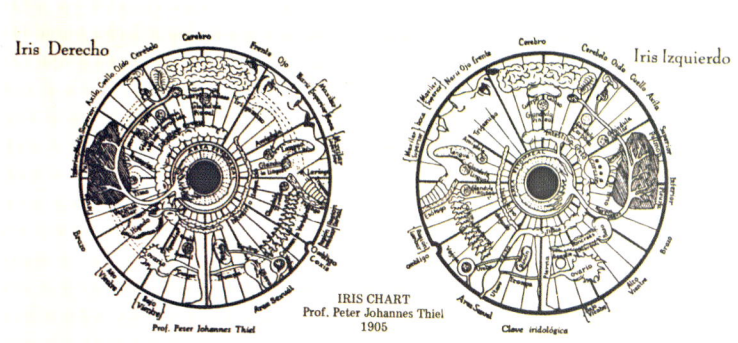

IRIDOLOGY CHARTS PAST AND PRESENT

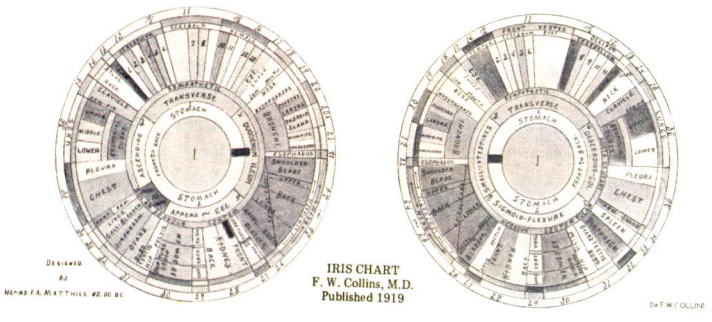

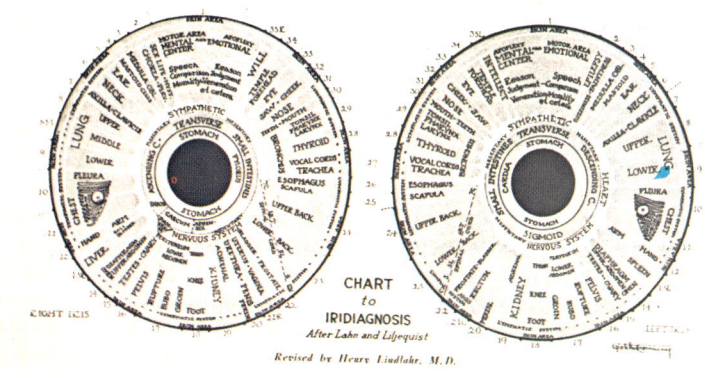

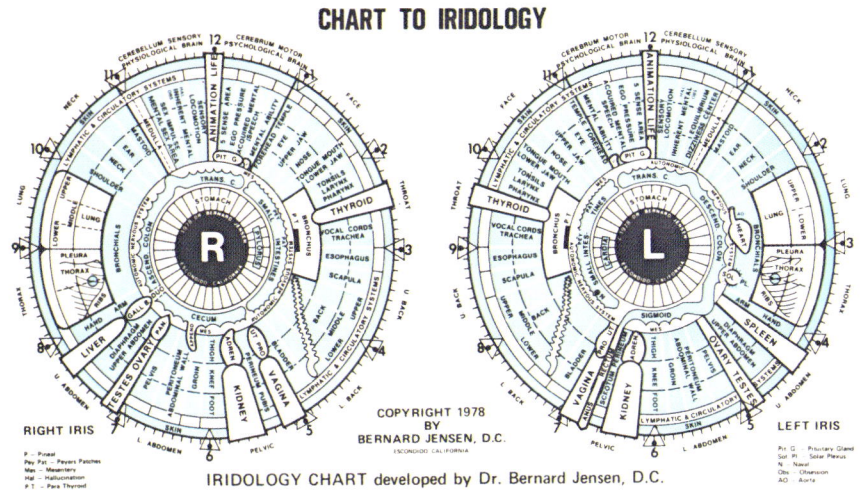

IRIDOLOGY CHART developed by Dr. Bernard Jensen, D.C.

NO TWO EYES ALIKE

No two eyes, as I have mentioned before, are alike. Now that does not mean there is no structural similarity, or iridology would not be possible. Nor does it mean there are no similarities among family members. We have done studies of the eyes of identical twins and identical triplets, and there are many common features, although there were also differences. We have also studied the eyes of three generations in families—grandparents, parents and children—and, again, found similarities and differences. In particular, we could see inherent weaknesses that passed down from one side of the family or the other, in the same organs or tissues. Studies such as these make a strong case for the validity of iridology.

The iris photo (following page) shows a wonderful constitution. Notice the fine structure of the iris fibers, how closely they are knit together, like silk. This man inherited a strong constitution from his parents. Such a person is seldom sick, and when he is, he gets over it quickly. The natural immune system is strong, the energy reserves are there.

The four lower photos show weaker constitutions. When these people get colds, they drag on and on. If the cold develops into pneumonia, they do not get their energy and vitality back for months, no matter what antibiotics their doctors give them. Because antibiotics kill the beneficial bacteria in the colon as well as pathogenic bacteria in the lungs and bronchial areas, they have an additional problem to cope with, along with general weakness and low vitality.

On the other hand, these people can get well and stay well too. These inherent weaknesses, the holes or lesions seen throughout these four irides, were acquired from birth. You will never have tissue like that unless you have been born that way.

A poor constitution does not indicate disease in the body, but only low resistance, low recuperative power.

If a person with a weak constitution reflexly indicated by an iris pattern as loosely and roughly woven as burlap keeps his

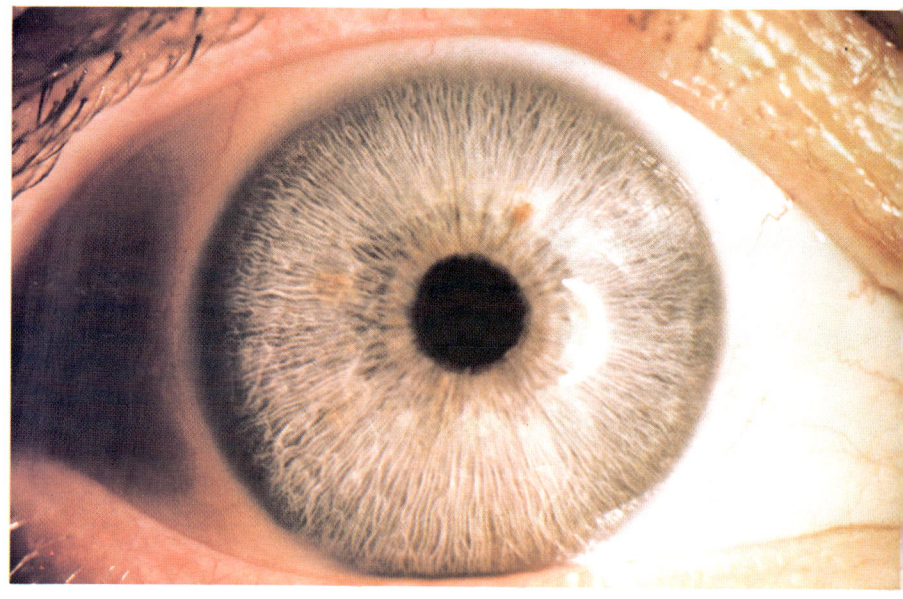

body clean, eats right, gets sufficient fresh air, exercise and rest, he can stay as well as the person with a strong constitution. The person with a strong constitution can eat anything and get away with it—to a point. The person with a weak constitution cannot. That is the difference.

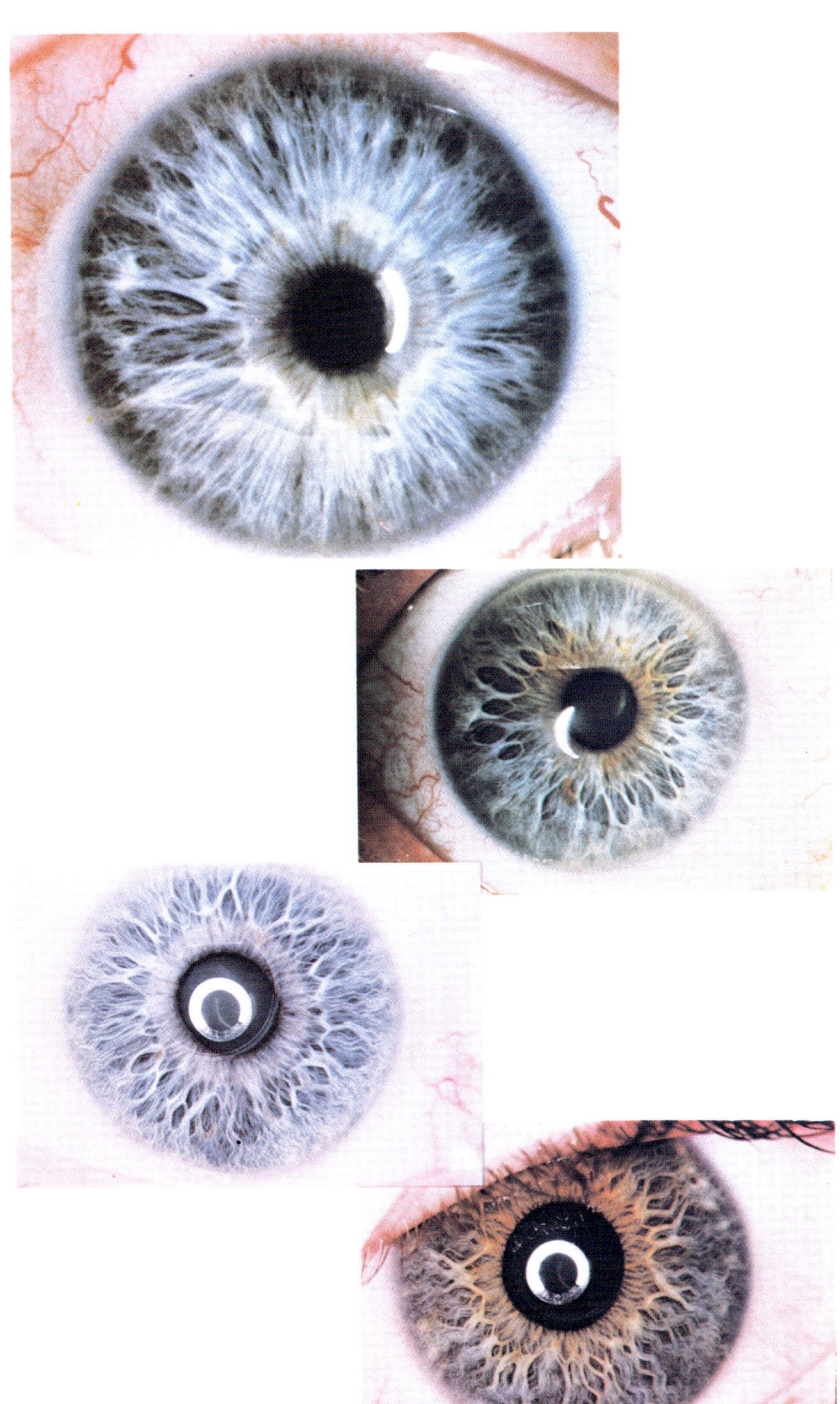

The value of knowing where the inherent weaknesses are in the body is considerable. As I said before, particular organs, glands and tissues in the body need certain chemical elements to stay healthy. If you know what minerals are needed, you can make sure your diet includes foods containing them. Inherently weak tissues are metabolically less active than other tissues, which means they need a higher intake of nutrients to sustain an adequate level of function.

Because people have different inherent weaknesses, poor care of the body may result in different symptom patterns or diseases. With a steady diet of coffee, donuts, hamburgers and French fries, one person may develop asthma, another arthritis and the third may get atherosclerosis. The same bad habits do not produce the same results in everyone. Good health habits, on the other hand, tend to build high-level well-being in all who follow them.

ENERGY PATTERNS

All the photographic subjects on the next page express energy patterns. Along the right side and bottom are Kirlian photographs showing energy fields, flow patterns and flares indicating differences in electrical potential, resistance and dielectric properties.

We all have patterns of energy flow in our bodies, but they differ just as fingerprints differ. The FBI has millions of fingerprints in Washington, DC, and each is unique. Similarly, the irides are different in everyone.

Next to the artistic renderings of the anatomy of the eye, the bottom three Kirlian pictures show energy flares surrounding dark spaces (the fingertips) that appear very similar to iris lesions or inherent weaknesses. The top two Kirlian photos on the right show interior energy patterns that remind me of the healing lines that come into dark lesions as tissue heals in the body.

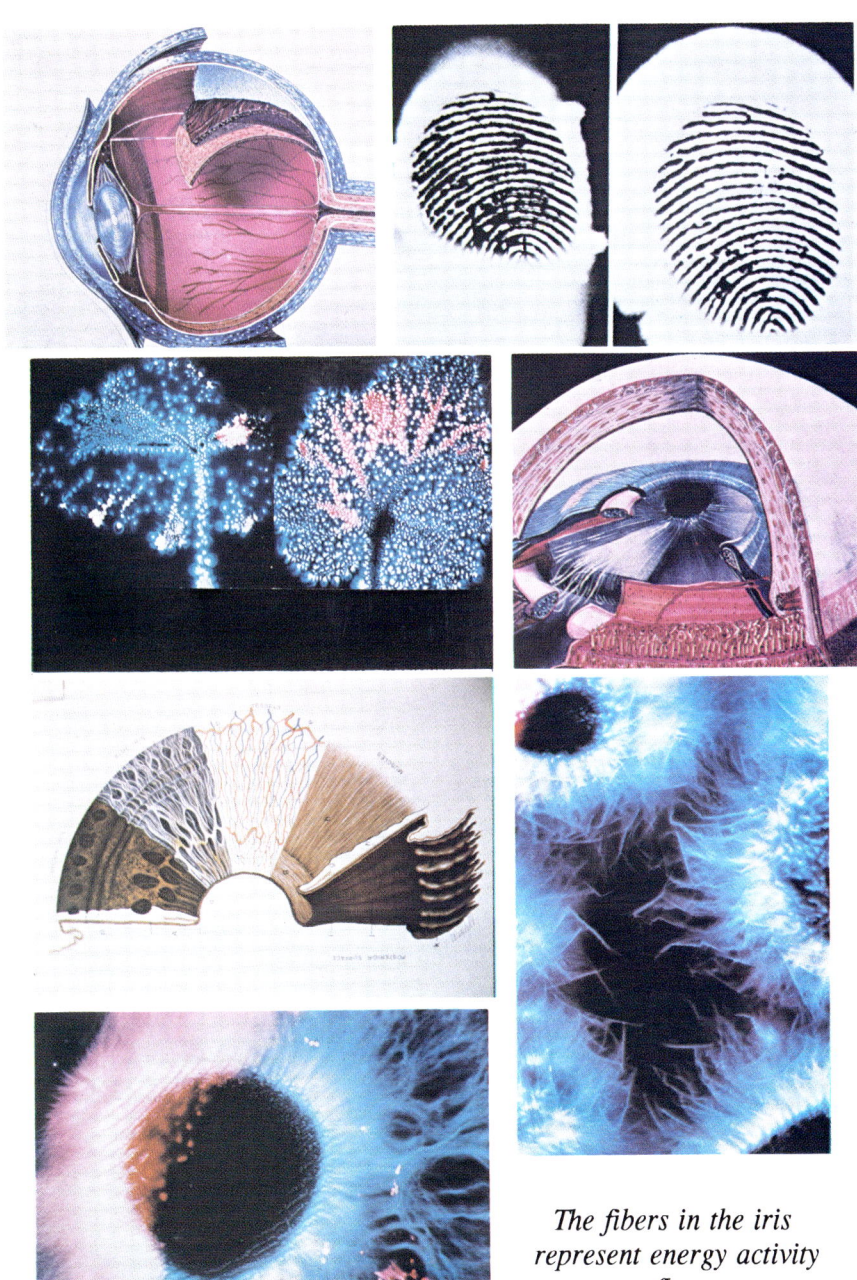

The fibers in the iris represent energy activity or energy flow.

Perhaps this is more than pure coincidence. Could the similarity between Kirlian filaments and iris fibers be based on similar patterns of energy flow? Dr. Hans Jenny, a Swiss physician, has demonstrated how sound frequencies create symmetrical energy patterns in liquids, powders and various viscous substances. Perhaps during the formation of the embryo in the mother's womb, the semi-liquid iris fibers are shaped and streamlined according to some genetic code, influenced to a degree by nutrition and other environmental factors, especially vibratory factors such as sound, rhythms within the mother's body and even higher frequency phenomena.

Another source of energy patterns in the iris is the rich network of nerve fibers, both sympathetic and parasympathetic that control the dilator and sphincter muscles and continue into the stroma, the main body of the iris. One ophthalmology text says, "...Every stromal cell and chromatophore receives its own nerve supply...." which would mean the iris is extremely sensitive to any alterations in nerve impulse patterns from the brain.

EYE PATTERNS

Physiology texts point out that the iris is composed of four primary layers: the anterior, the stroma, the muscle (which dilates or constricts the pupil) and the posterior pigment epithelium. The stroma—or main body of the iris—determines eye color and contains a network of fine, white radial fibers. Under magnification, these are seen to be arranged in vascular arcades three or four layers deep.

When the iris fibers become separated, a "hole" is created. The degree of darkness perceived depends upon how many layers deep the hole or lesion is. The deeper they are, the darker they appear, since the dark pigment epithelium becomes more exposed.

Brown eyes are due to the presence of melanin pigment cells in the stroma, while blue eyes obtain their color from light reflected off the posterior epithelial layer of the iris. In the latter, the stroma is clear. All other eye colors are due to inherited mixtures from brown- and blue-eyed parents, with the exception of color changes due to drugs.

To the iridologist, the degree of fine or coarse structure in the iris is an indication of constitutional strength or weakness. Fine-grained oak is much stronger than coarse-grained pine, but both serve their purpose well if taken care of properly. The same holds true of those with strong or weak constitutions. We differentiate between the two by saying that those with strong constitutions show greater resistance to disease and faster recovery times if they get some ailment.

Notice the dark eye in the picture below. The circular bands most prominent on the right side are called nerve rings. Under magnification, these are seen as actual furrows in the surface of the iris, and researchers have found that identical matching furrows are located in the posterior pigment epithelium. Iridologists use them to evaluate an individual's degree of stress.

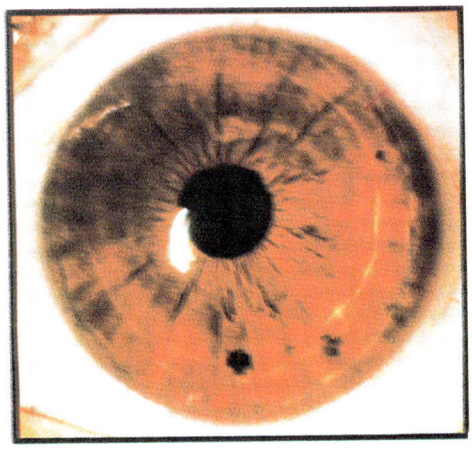

Notice the lesions in the iris below. The darker the lesion, the older the problem. The darkest lesions are the most chronic, many of them dating back to childhood. In general, I find the darkest area in the great majority of irides to be in the bowel area; and the bronchial areas, 2 to 4 o'clock in the left iris, 8 to 10 o'clock in the right, are often almost as dark. This, I believe, is because we do not eat the right foods and we do not take proper care of the bowel. A sluggish bowel or a pocketed condition of the bowel, as in diverticulosis, can cause problems elsewhere in the body.

The American Cancer Society has said that it takes as long as 20 years to develop cancer. It does not come overnight. It does not come from a single cigarette. You have to work to create a chronic condition. You have to eat it, drink it, think it, worry it into existence. Symptom-suppressing drugs compound the problem, driving the basic cause more deeply into the tissues. We see this in iridology as the lesions grow darker in time when no corrective measures are taken. We should never suppress colds, flu or other catarrhal conditions. Let it flow. Let the body get rid of it as nature intended; otherwise, we develop congestion in the body.

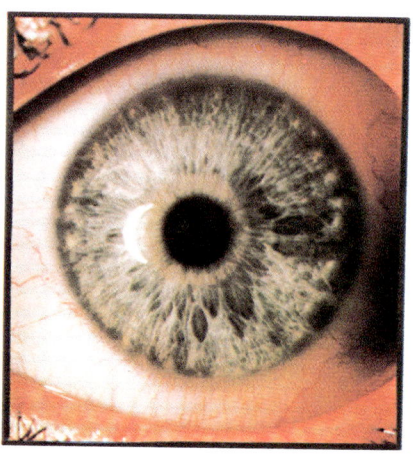

When the iris fibers are white, we can say there is a problem with congestion, with excessive acidity in the body, but we cannot say this person has asthma, hay fever or bronchitis. Keep in mind that we are always looking at tissue conditions, not the symptomatic outcome of those conditions nor diseases in themselves. Signs of congestion in the iris indicate underactivity in the tissues, lack of vital force, deficiencies in specific minerals. We have to understand basic facts about nutrition to deal with these conditions intelligently.

The ring circling the pupil in the picture below is a chronic acid stomach ring, indicating a deficiency in hydrochloric acid. Who can digest foods well without it? This is the sort of thing

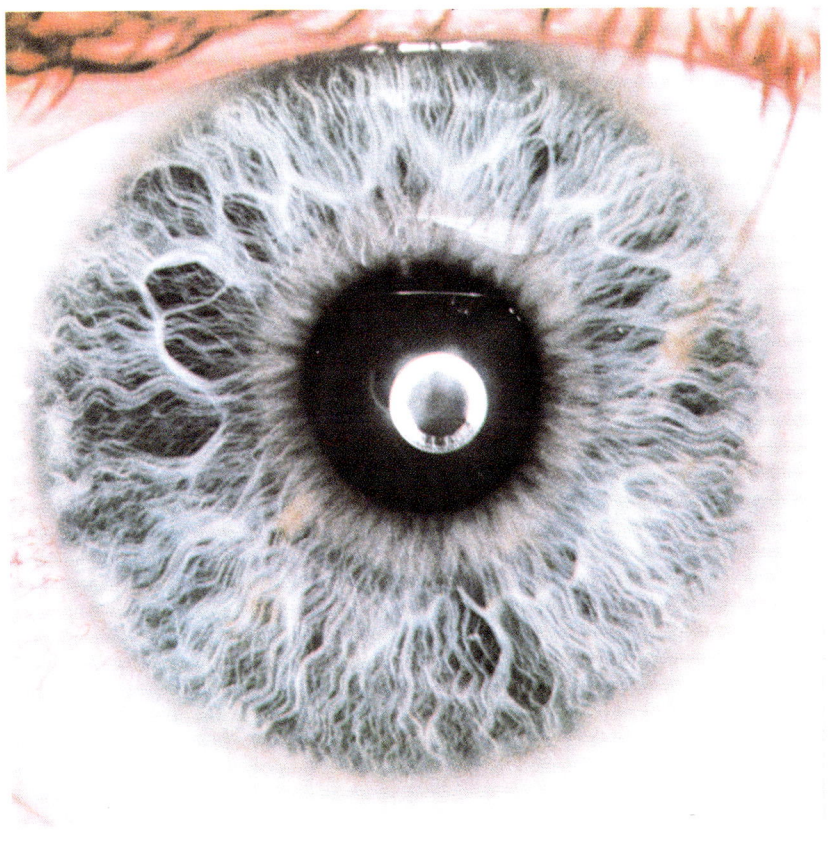

we must correct, since any impediment to digestion or assimilation interferes with nutrition, leaving the body just as undernourished as if the diet itself was deficient. One of the first steps in taking care of anyone with a chronic condition is to make sure the digestion and assimilation are functioning normally.

Iris patterns are as unique as fingerprints and personalities, expressing the individual makeup of each person's body, its strengths and weaknesses.

HEALING SIGNS

The large iris photo on the following page provides an excellent demonstration of a beautiful fiber structure. I want you to notice especially the cross fibers in the two large lesions between 2 and 3 o'clock. These are healing signs. They show the patient is making a change for the better in the lung structure.

The large size of the pupil indicates fatigue, enervation, tiredness; and we often find a kind of wavy fiber structure when we have a pupil of that size. But those healing signs are very good news for the patient. They come in when we get away from the snack foods, fried foods, junk foods and start eating properly, start getting enough rest, start exercising. We have to work to bring in these healing signs.

Iridology is a master art for telling whether the doctor and his patient are on the right track or not. No one has any business working with patients unless the patients are getting better, making a better body with new tissue replacing the old.

In the lower picture, we see an illustration showing Hering's law of cure as it applies in the iris. Arrows 1, 2, 3 and 4 indicate, respectively, acute, subacute, chronic and degenerative stages of tissue damage, the iris lesion growing deeper and darker with each stage. Arrows 5, 6, 7 and 8 show the reversal

HERING'S LAW OF CURE AS IT APPLIES IN THE IRIS OF THE EYE
Levels or depth of disruption or k
ting of fibers are shown individu
for clarity & in actual analysis, th
may be in varying degree
combinations of ab
ACUTE
SUBACUTE
CHRONIC
DESTROYED
Progression toward chronic disease as indicated by , , , representing stages or depth of disruption of fibers in iris.
Progression toward healing as indicated by knitting of fibers at different levels shown by , , , and .

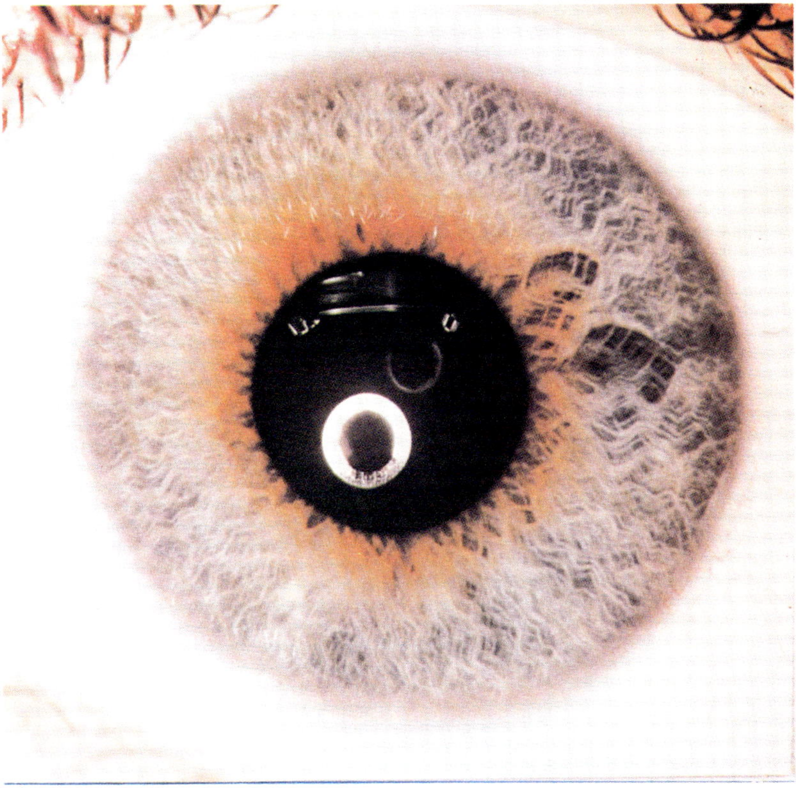

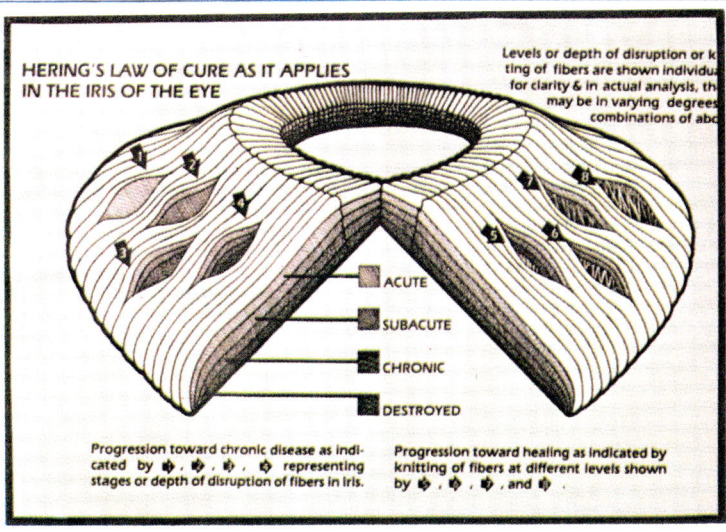

path brought about by changing to a healthy way of life. Healing lines are coming "from the inside out." This is when the healing crisis comes. This is when the natural immune system, the organs and tissues, the strength and vitality are restored sufficiently to force out the old catarrh and toxins, to throw off the cause of the disease, to clean out the body.

We work for cleanliness, and we find the degree of cleanliness in any particular inherently weak organ, gland or tissue is evident by the state of activity (degenerative, chronic, subacute or acute), ranging in shades from black (degenerative) to white (acute).

It is not a matter of just getting rid of the pain, which is a wonderful art in itself, but nutrition brings healing, and healing eventually relieves the pain and discomfort permanently.

Today, the medical profession pays little attention to nutrition, but I believe the tide may be turning. Men like the late Dr. Alan Nittler, MD, who wrote *A New Breed of Doctor*, have done marvelous things for patients with foods. Dr., Bieler of Pasadena, another MD who really knows his nutrition. Many years ago, I went to see Dr. Bieler about the tremendous results I was getting with nutrition. He tried it, and when he saw the nice changes that were happening to his patients, he started using food as a medicine. His book, *Food Is Your Medicine*, is a wonderful testimony to the effectiveness of nutrition.

LEGS

In the top photo (following two pages), you will notice an ulcer above the anklebone. Now these do not come about overnight, and they do not appear at all if the person has a balanced nutritional intake, but there are several things we can learn from this case.

Looking at the two legs, we see they are not only unequal in size, but somewhat different shape as well.

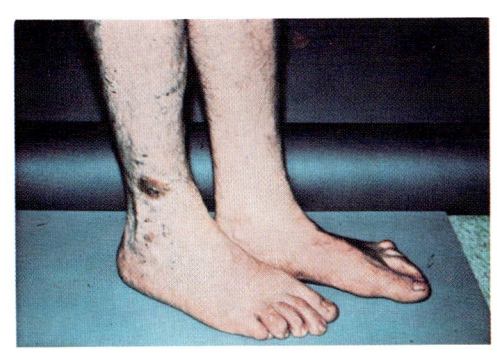

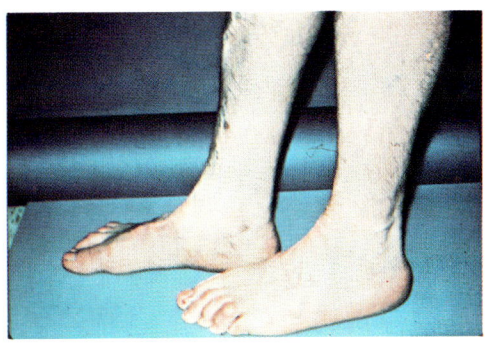

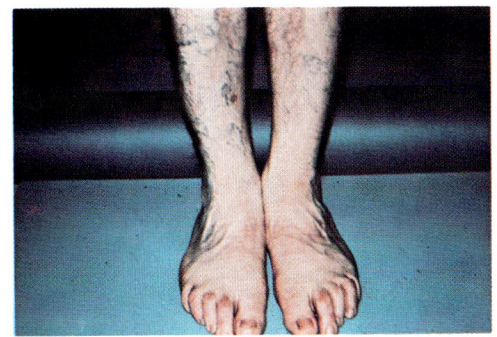

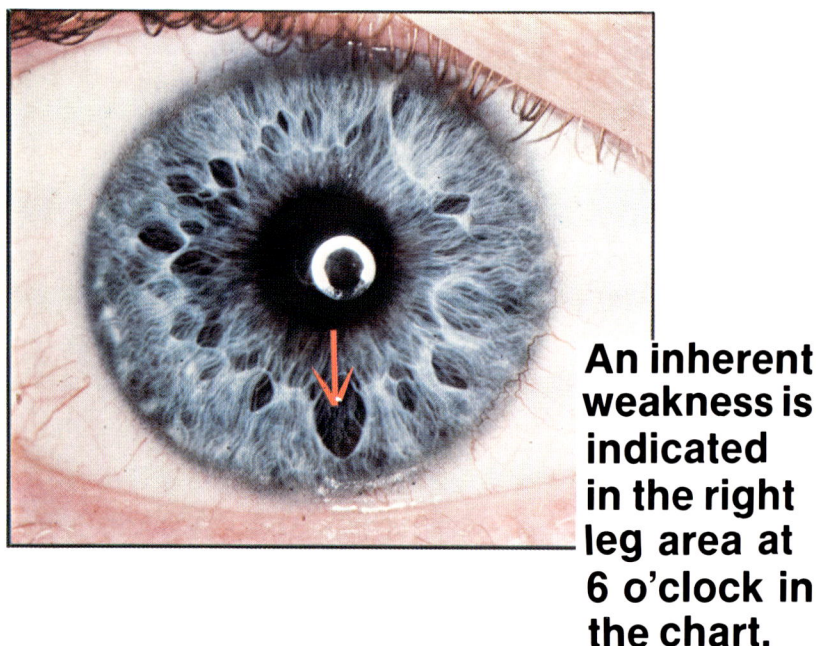

An inherent weakness is indicated in the right leg area at 6 o'clock in the chart.

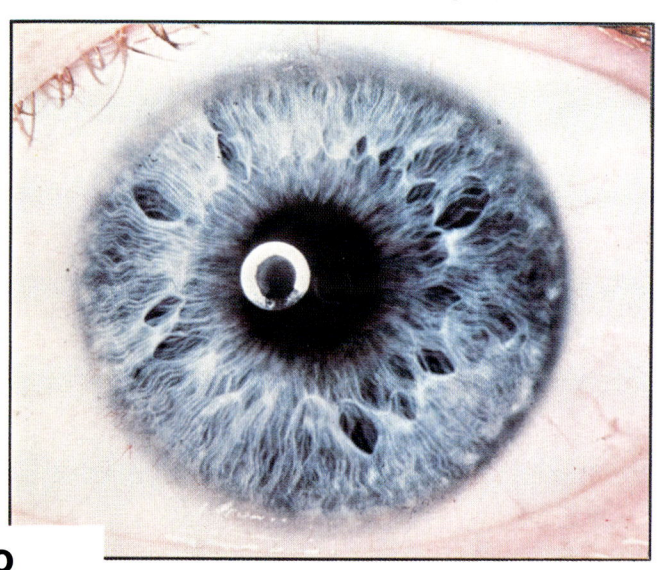

Note no comparable lesion in left leg area of chart.

Compare the color of the veins in the right leg with those in the left. Can you see how much bluer they are in the right leg?

Now let us go to the eye. At 6 o'clock, we find the leg area, starting with the foot near the outside perimeter of the chart. Notice the large lesion or hole in the right iris, indicating inherent weakness in the tissue of the right leg. We can define inherent weakness as metabolic deficiency; inherently weak tissue does not assimilate nutrients or eliminate metabolic wastes as efficiently as normal or inherently strong tissue, so it is more vulnerable to various diseases and ailments.

Shifting to the left iris, we encounter no lesions in the leg area, although there are other inherent weaknesses to be seen, just as there are in the right iris. A person who has inherent weaknesses can remain healthy if he or she takes care to live right.

The degree of darkness of the lesion determines whether we classify the tissue area as acute, subacute, chronic or degenerative, the last being the darkest, least active and usually the most long-term condition.

BACK AREA: RIGHT AND LEFT IRIDES

Back problems of various kinds are among the most common complaints brought to doctors, and some of these conditions become chronic and extremely painful, despite the best efforts of medical science.

All the eyes on the following page show back problems. We always examine the back area in both irides because each iris carries information from the nerves on its own side of the body, and what we find differs on the right and left.

Notice the dark lesions in the back area. Most people who have black lesions in the back area of the iris complain of backaches. What it generally indicates is lack of calcium, aside from any other problems with nerves, muscles, ligaments or spine.

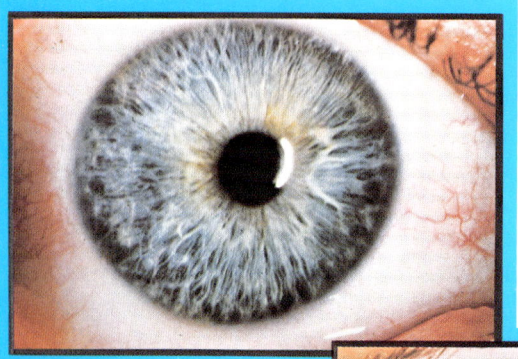

BACK AREA: RIGHT IRIS

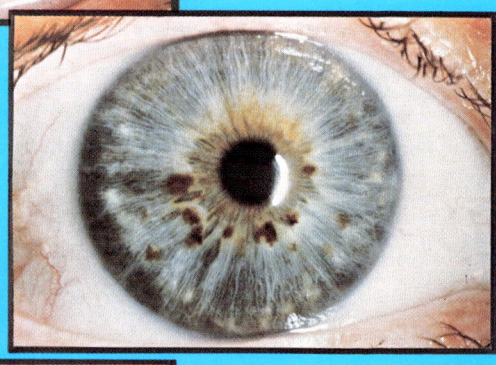

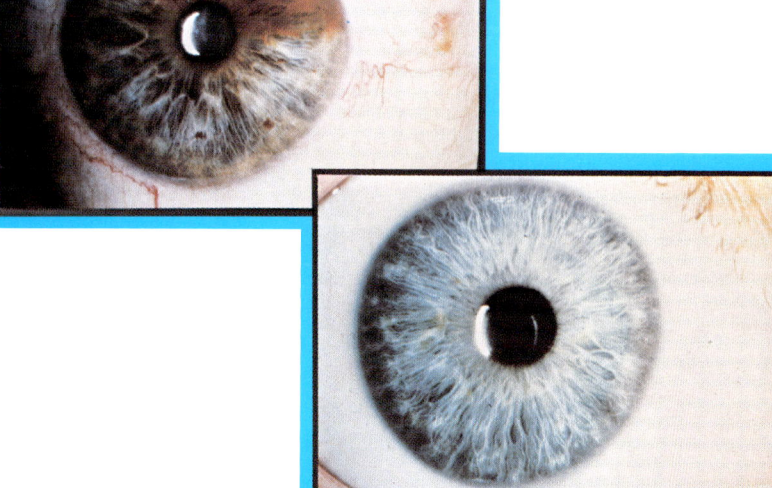

**BACK AREA:
RIGHT IRIS**

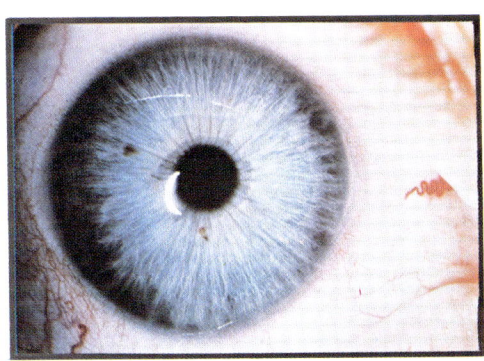

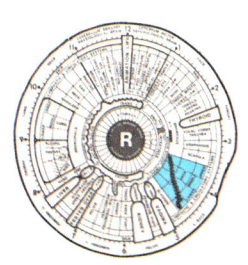
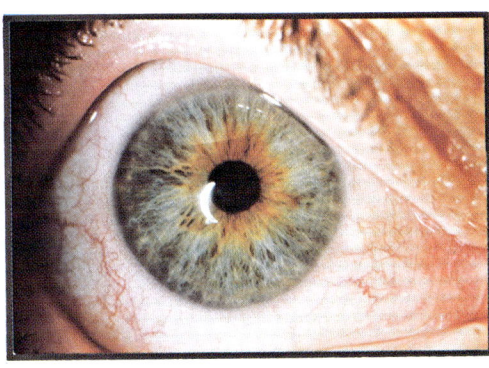

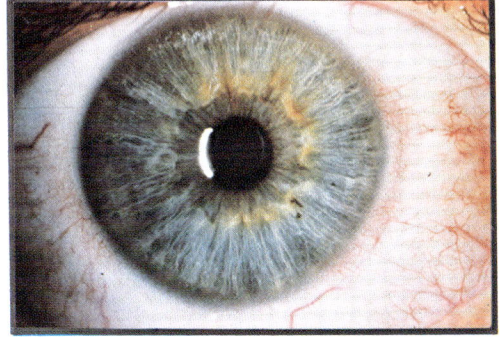

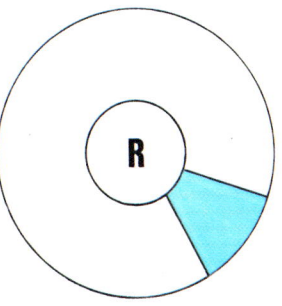

BACK AREA: LEFT IRIS

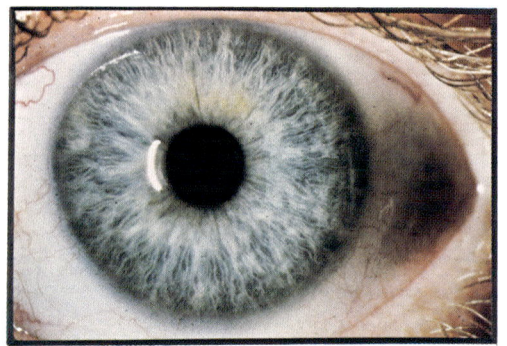

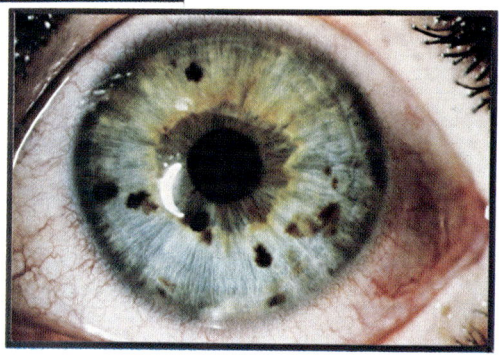

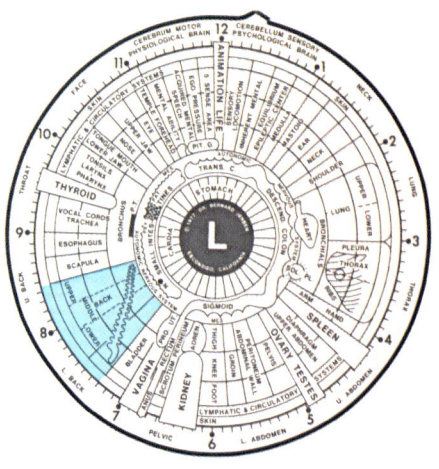

BACK AREA: LEFT IRIS (Continued)

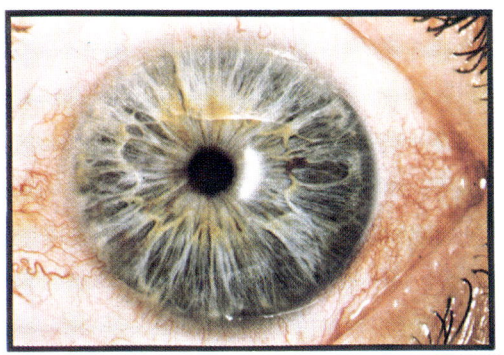

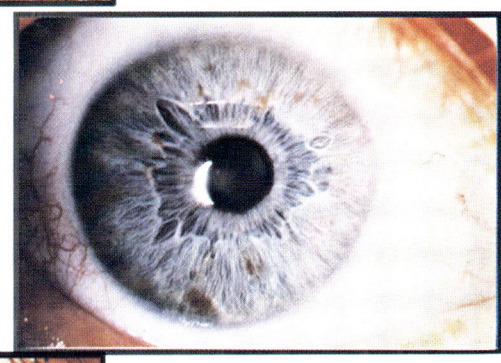

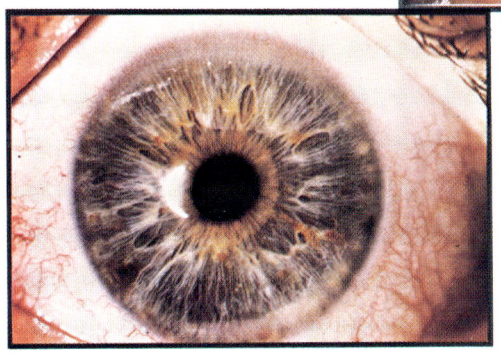

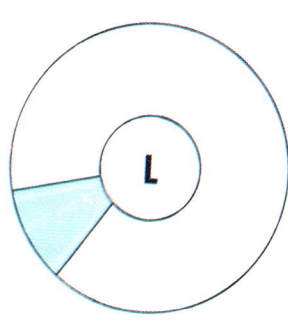

KIDNEY AREA: RIGHT IRIS

Here we see inherent weaknesses of the right kidney. If we do not push an inherently weak kidney too hard, it will last and do a good job. Basically, the kidney is a highly-efficient filtration system, designed to sort out waste products from nutrients and minerals the body needs to recycle. If kidney malfunction allows the level of a metabolic waste product such as urea to become too high in the bloodstream, we are in trouble. A toxic condition develops in the body, diminishing the performance level of every tissue—including the brain. Often, the source of the problem is the kidneys, but it is also true that the problem may have begun elsewhere, creating an excessive workload on the kidneys.

One way this can happen is if the other eliminative organs and systems: bowel, lymph, lungs and skin are not doing their share of work. When one or more of these eliminative outlets is impeded or sluggish, more waste is diverted to the kidneys. The kidneys have to take care of the "overflow," and the additional stress can damage the kidney nephrons.

Acid foods, alcohol, junk foods and even worry or mental overwork can break down the kidneys. Iridology often indicates trouble before physical symptoms begin, allowing preventative steps to be taken in time to avoid serious problems.

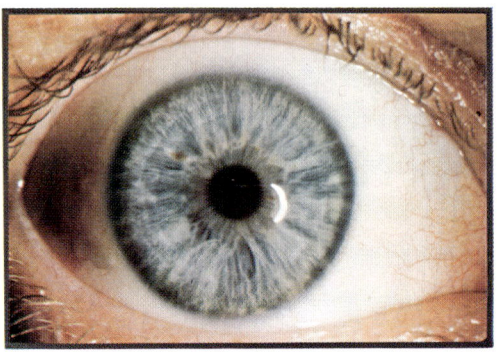
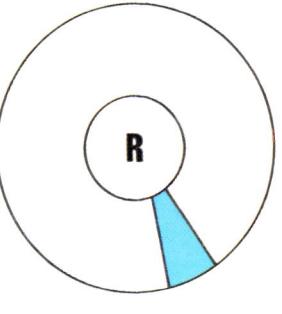

KIDNEY AREA: RIGHT IRIS

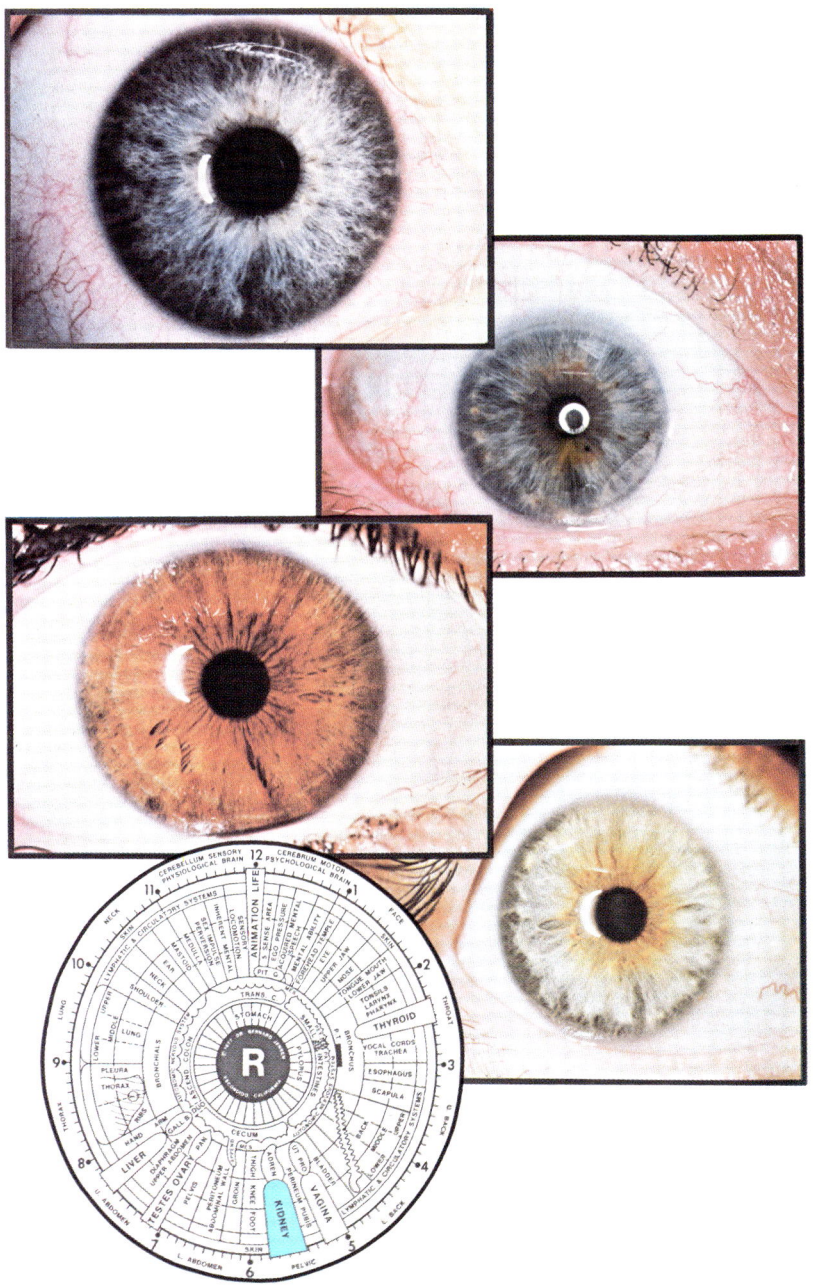

KIDNEY AREA: LEFT IRIS

One of the most useful aspects of iridology is its ability to distinguish whether one or both of any bilateral organs or glands is functionally impaired. Bilateral organs and glands include the kidneys, testes, ovaries, adrenals, lungs and thyroid. Blood and urine tests cannot make this distinction, and once a problem is identified in a bilateral system by means of these tests, further medical tests to isolate which gland or organ is involved, or to determine whether both are involved, can be painful, expensive and dangerous.

Iridology can immediately and painlessly reveal whether the right kidney, the left kidney or both are functionally impaired. In many cases, I believe iridology indicates trouble at the preclinical stage, before conventional tests show anything abnormal and before any symptoms appear.

Another advantage of iridology is its capacity for tracing interrelated problems. There is no such thing as a pathological problem isolated in one organ. Usually conditions which cause trouble in one organ will cause trouble in others, not to the same extent perhaps, but it is important to know these things in order to respond to them appropriately. If a problem in the bowel is reflexly irritating the left kidney, it is useless to treat only the kidney. The kidney condition will simply reappear over and over, to the frustration of both patient and doctor. But, if we take care of the bowel problem, the kidney symptoms will vanish.

In general, if any of the eliminative systems is impaired or underactive, one or more of the other elimination systems can become overloaded, overstressed, creating a problem there, too.

KIDNEY AREA: LEFT IRIS

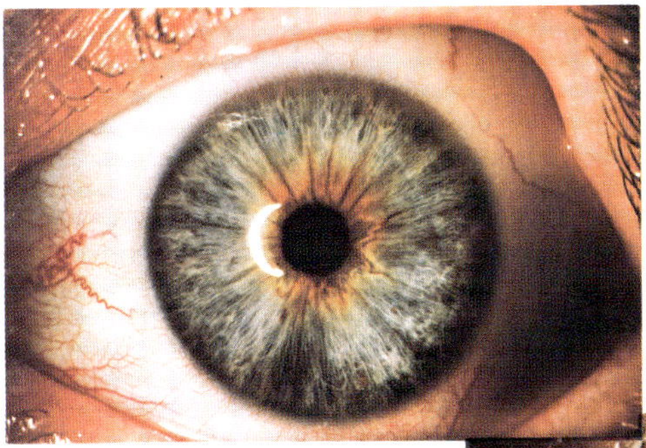

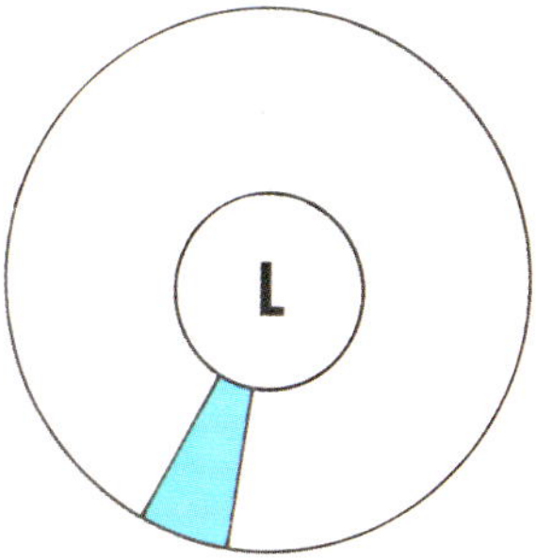

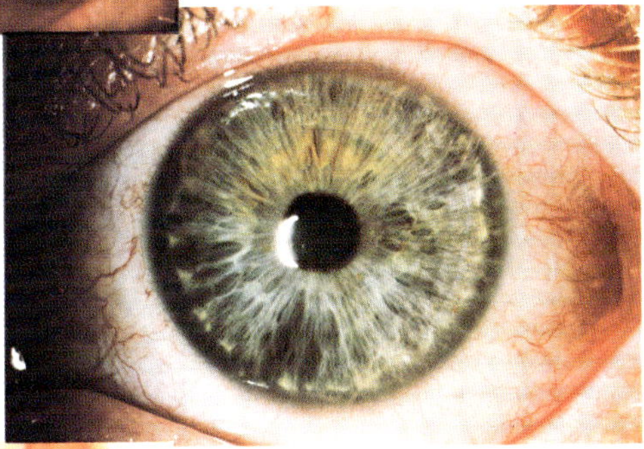

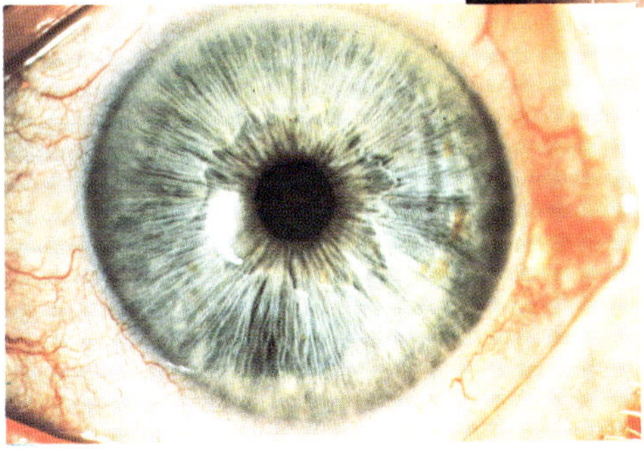

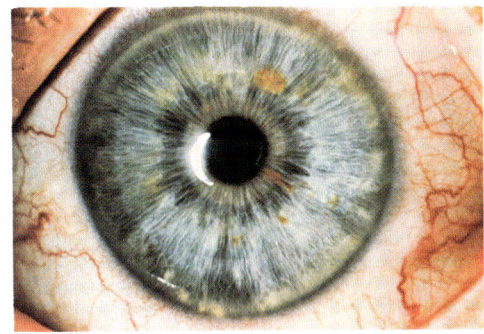

KIDNEY AREA: LEFT IRIS

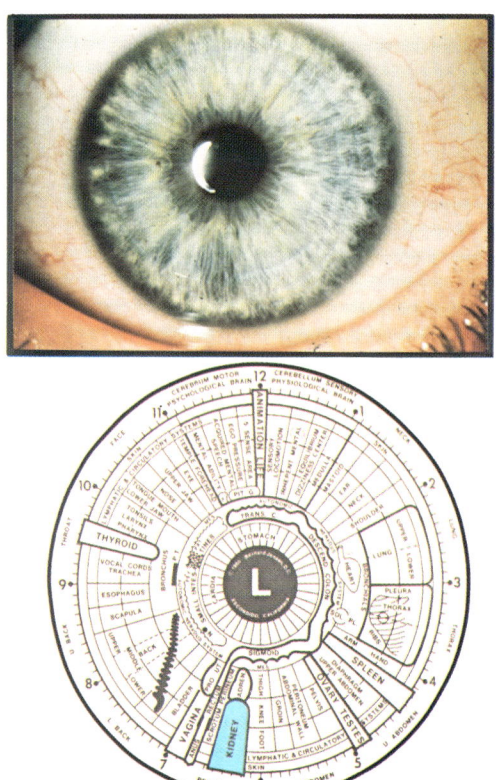

RESPIRATORY AREA: RIGHT IRIS

Like the kidneys, the lungs are bilateral organs, and iridology can show whether the right respiratory area or the left or both are overactive or underactive.

Between 9 and 10 o'clock on the Iridology Chart and in the iris, we find the lung structure and just inside it, toward the pupil, we see the bronchials. If this area shows white, irritated iris fibers, we know there is an acute condition, an overactivity which usually indicates a running catarrhal condition. If it is dark, we know the catarrh is not running, not moving.

In working with natural laws and natural principles, we would not advise, generally, suppression of a discharge because this is the body's natural means of getting rid of toxic material. Suppressing symptoms simply drives the catarrh and toxins back into the tissues. This creates an even more dangerous situation than before, because it forces a toxic irritant to remain in contact with vital, living tissue.

When we find dark lesions in the lung and bronchial areas, a program is needed to awaken and strengthen these tissues in order to liquefy and throw off the toxic material settled there. As this liquefying takes place, the catarrh begins to run and familiar symptoms develop—running nose, fever, coughing and so forth. This is the "healing crisis" which the natural healing arts hold in such high esteem.

Dr. Henry Lindlahr once said, "Give me a healing crisis and I will cure any disease." We have strengthened the body to a level where it is able to throw off the material causing the problem, and this is the most effective way of taking care of the human body. It is nature's way. Healing crises are usually short and intense, perhaps three days, and they come immediately after the patient has worked his or her way to a peak of well-being through right eating and right living.

I am quite familiar with the healing crisis, because I have spent 50 years working with patients in my sanitariums. Some patients have come in with very little life left in their bodies. Many times I have sat up all night, spoon-feeding them with whey or broth every half hour, just to bring these people back. I love to watch them come back. This is the biggest reward a doctor can receive—watching his patients getting well and strong again.

RESPIRATORY AREA: RIGHT IRIS

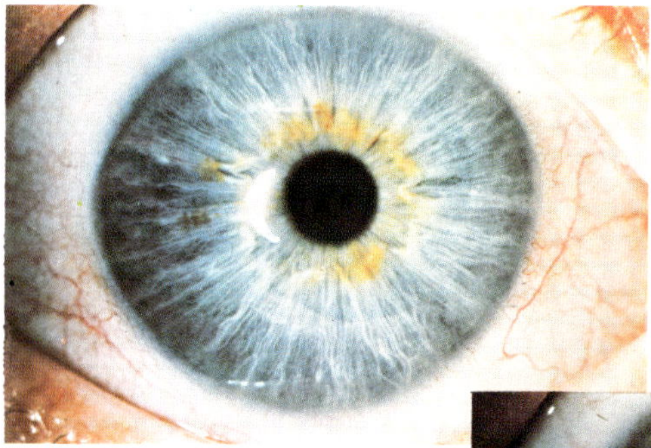

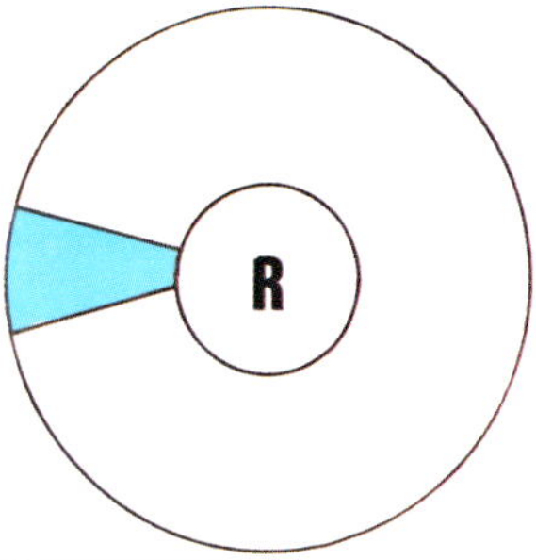

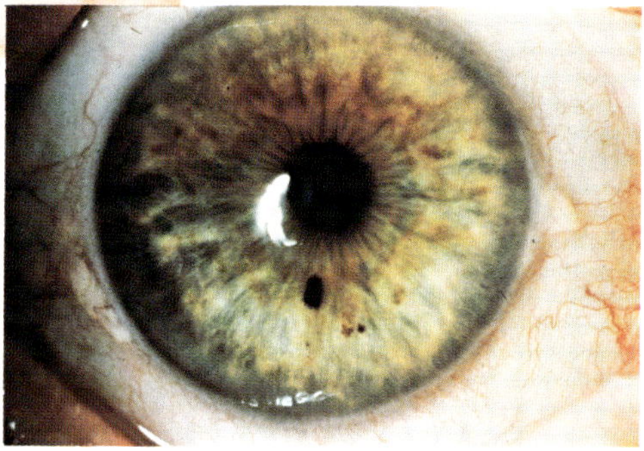

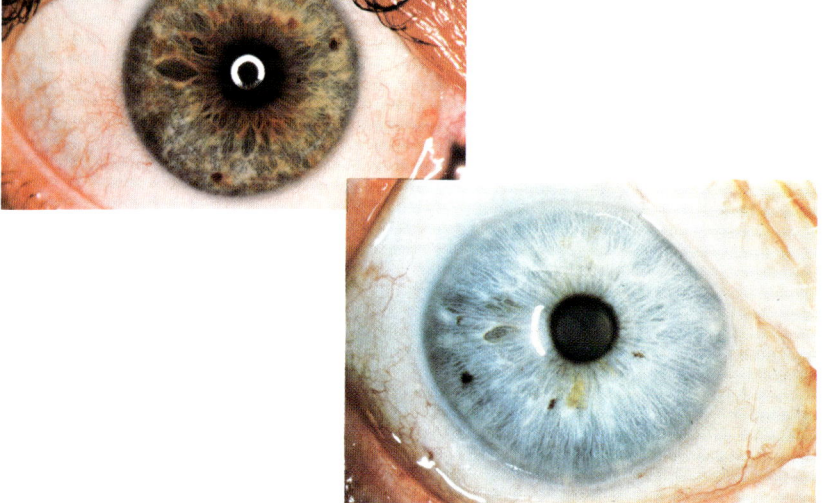

RESPIRATORY AREA: RIGHT IRIS

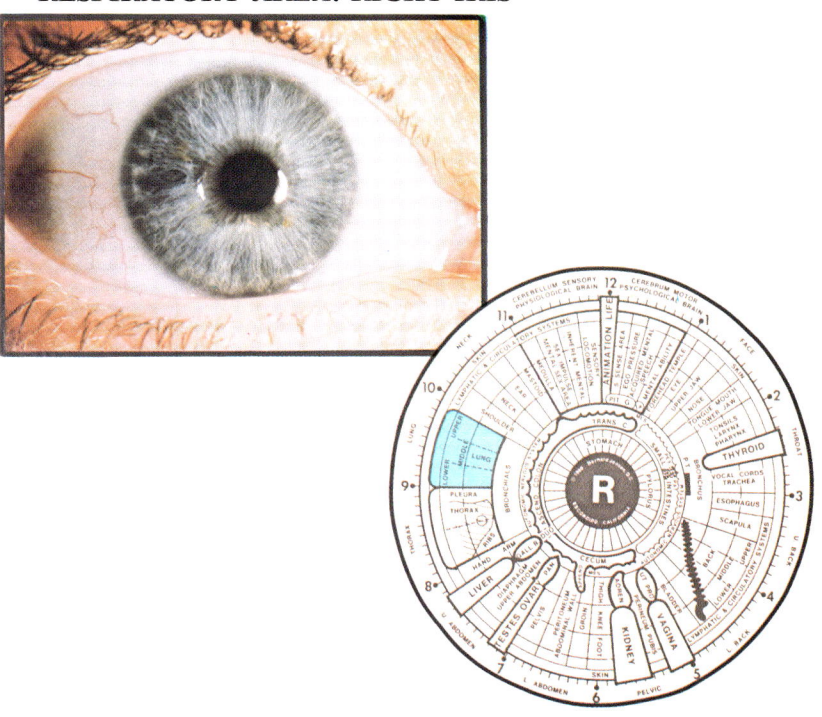

RESPIRATORY AREA: LEFT IRIS

Now we are going to the left respiratory area, and I want to point out something that has meant a great deal in my work. Notice that in the iris, the left bronchial area is adjacent to the descending colon, inside the autonomic nerve wreath which circles the pupil a short distance away from it. In the right iris, the bronchials are next to the ascending colon.

Many years ago, I noticed the darkest area of the irides was usually the colon area. Often, however, the bronchial and lung

RESPIRATORY AREA: LEFT IRIS

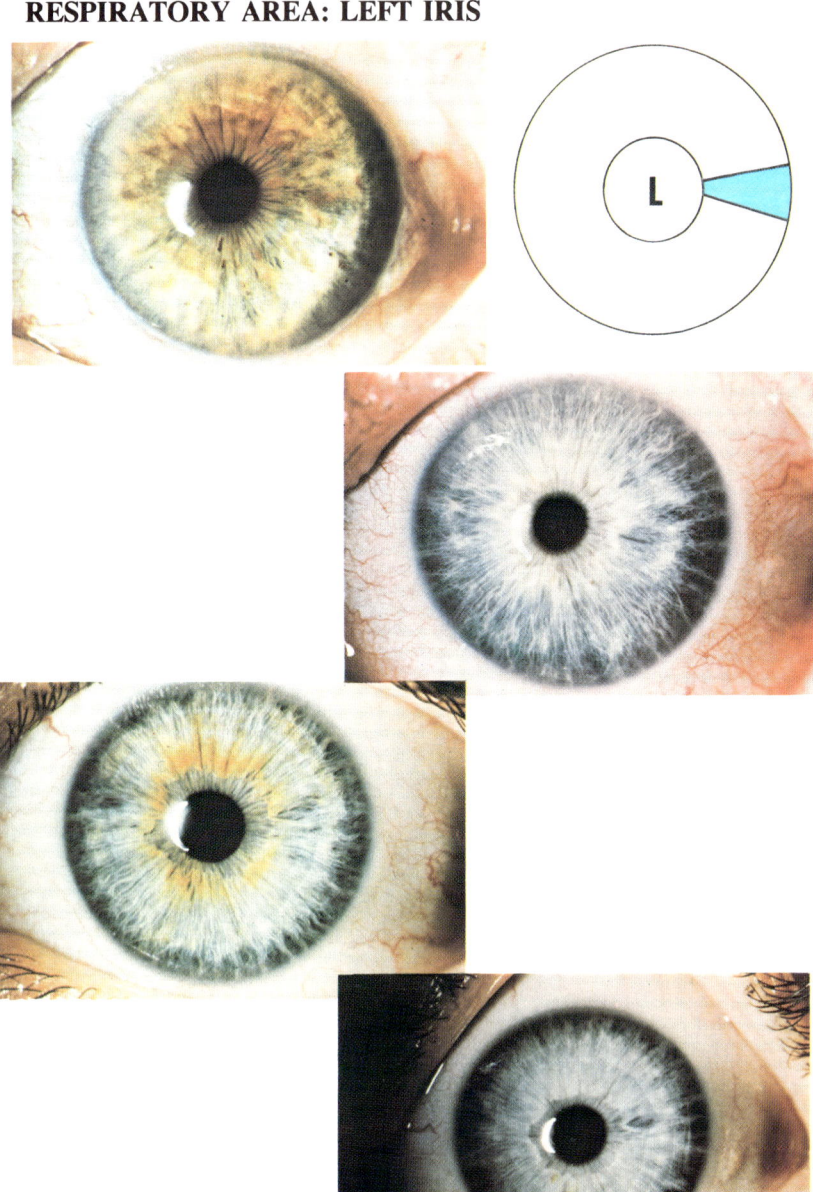

RESPIRATORY AREA: LEFT IRIS

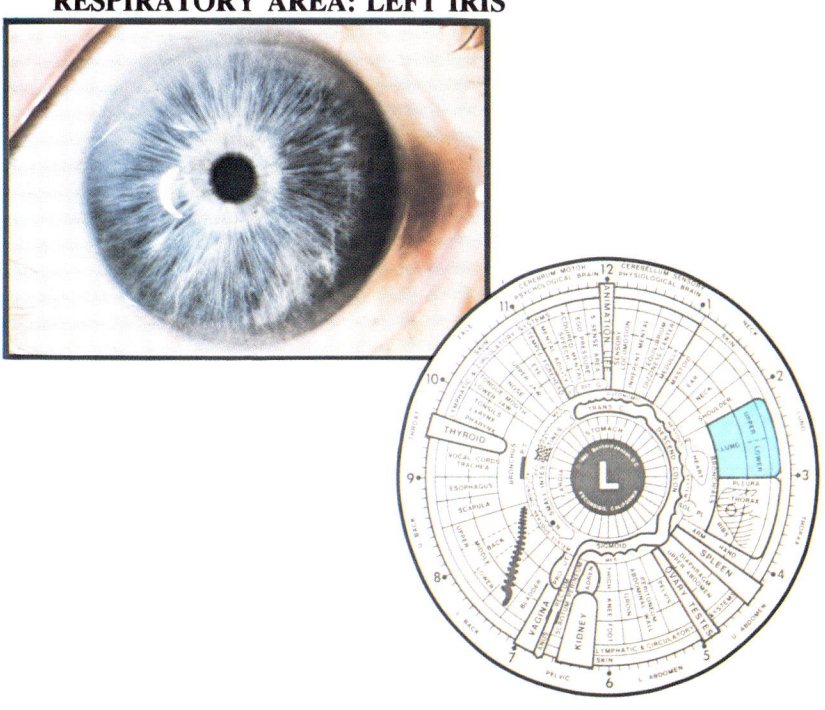

areas were almost as dark. I wondered if there was any relationship between the bowel and the lungs which could be triggering symptoms in the lungs and bronchials.

Further study and experience showed the existence of some kind of neural reflex through which toxins picked up by the bloodstream from the bowel were making their way into the lung structure. The British surgeon Sir Arbuthnot Lane discovered the same thing when he removed a pocketed section of the colon from an asthmatic patient. The asthma cleared up within a few weeks. He had many experiences of this kind. Researchers at the University of California in San Francisco have discovered a link between chronic constipation and breast cancer. So, I know I have found something here.

Respiratory problems can be inherited. A little lady came to me, and I told her she had inherited serious inherent weaknesses in both respiratory areas. "I am not surprised," she said, "my mother had bronchitis most of her life, and dad died of emphysema." This was in front of a class. There was no talk between us beforehand. The eyes tend to speak for themselves.

IT WORKS!

Val George first came to my Ranch in 1977, a 27-year-old man previously diagnosed by doctors at a V.A. Hospital as having such an advanced case of kidney disease (glomerulonephritis) that there was nothing they could do for him. He was sent home after being told he had only a few weeks to live, but he refused to give up.

Upon his arrival at my Ranch, Val was 52 pounds overweight due to water retention in the tissues. Notice (from the following photographs) the edema in his hands and abdomen. This is one of the symptoms that often accompany kidney disease.

My first iris analysis showed the most chronic and degenerative lesions to be in the bowel and kidney areas. Val told of his childhood years living on a farm, drinking a great deal of cow's milk and eating a lot of starchy foods. These had produced a heavy catarrhal condition that his elimination system could not handle. During his teen years and early 20s, Val's diet was overbalanced with what we call "junk" foods, which further contributed to a sluggish bowel condition and led to the breakdown of his inherently weak kidneys. Just as the weakest link in a chain breaks first under strain, the weakest organ, gland or tissue in the body breaks down first when we are not eating and living properly. The iris reveals these weakest links.

Usually when a patient's body is loaded with catarrh and toxic material, I advise an elimination diet or a fast with liquids only. In Val's case, this would have been too much for the kidneys to take, so I put him on a heavy eating program with a good deal of exercise and physical work. In 30 days he lost 32 pounds and felt better than he had in many years.

On the 31st day, he developed a healing crisis. A healing crisis is just like the disease crisis except for two telltale signs. A healing crisis usually comes after a peak period of excellent health, and it generally lasts only about three days. Val's body was built up to the point where it was strong enough to get rid of a good deal of the old catarrh and toxic material stored in the tissues.

The discharge in Val's case came through the bowel. He had 3 days of diarrhea, averaging 30 bowel movements in each 24-hour period. In this time, he lost another 12 pounds, although he gained 4 or 5 pounds back in the following days.

On the following pages, we show Val's hands at his bloated tissue condition and after his healing crisis. The lower pictures show his bloated stomach before and his stomach after. The irides pictures show the many fine healing lines coming in.

At this writing, it is now 6 years since Val George was given up to die, and he reports feeling wonderful. He works; is physically active; and enjoys a normal family life.

Iridology, we must realize, did not enable me to diagnose Val's glomerulonephritis. Analysis of his irides simply showed hypoactivity of the bowel (black, degenerative) and a related chronic condition of the kidneys (dark gray), with underactivity of the bronchials and skin as complicating factors.

I want to emphasize that Val was born with the inherent weaknesses we see in his eyes, but actual organ breakdown did not occur until wrong living habits brought it on. The lesions in his irides showed that breakdown coming as they became darker and darker. After he was put on a healthy living regimen, Hering's law of cure came into operation, tissues began to repair, and a healing crisis came to throw off the old and make way for the new. Iridology allows prediction of healing crises because we see the white healing lines coming in, and we know this means the body is growing strong enough to throw off old catarrh and toxic material on its own. Iridology tells us our

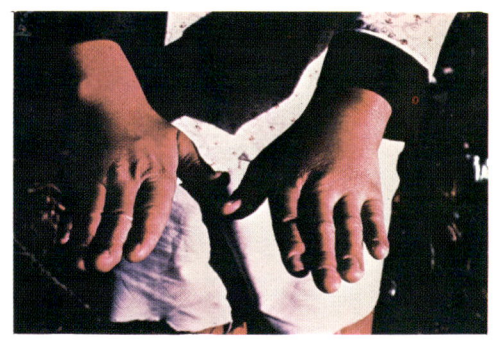

BEFORE

AFTER

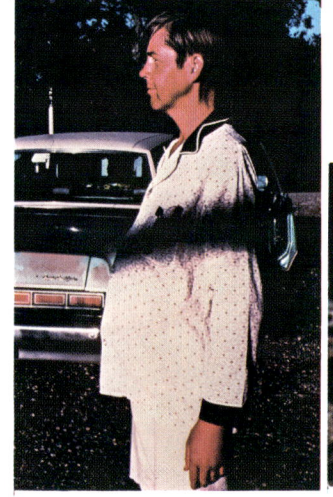

BEFORE

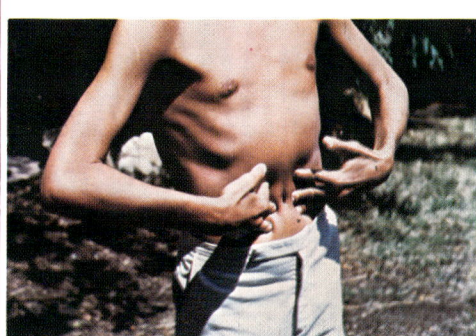

AFTER

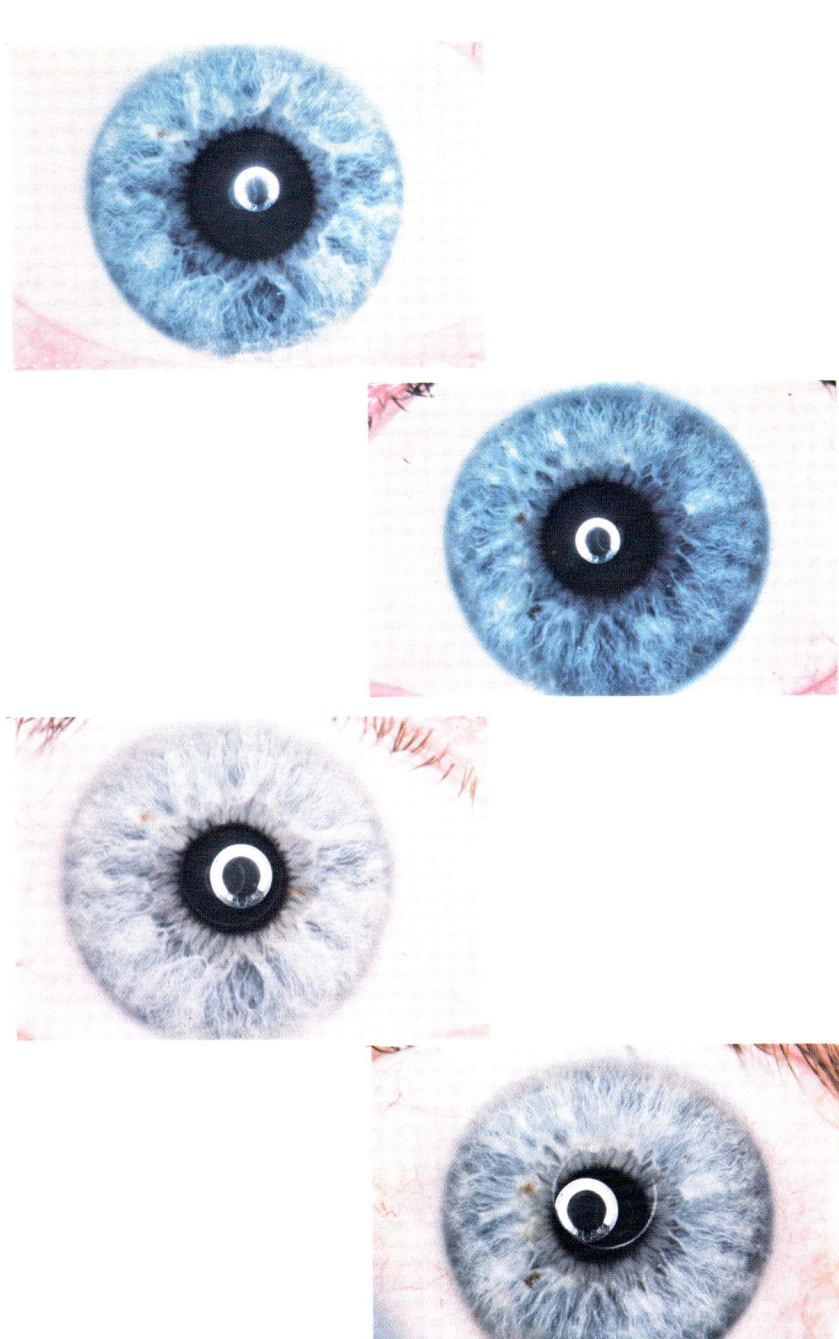

program or therapy is working, and this is one of the greatest things about it.

I might add that it made no difference whatsoever to know what other doctors diagnosed in Val George's case. On the basis of the iris analysis alone, I would have put him on the same program we actually used in 1977, and the same healing crisis would have occurred. In Val's third healing crisis, he brought up a great deal of catarrh and phlegm from the lungs and bronchial tubes, showing that the elimination systems, one by one, were being cleansed and renewed. He had bronchitis as a young child, and we see that the reversal of symptoms mentioned in Hering's law of cure even reaches back to childhood.

THROUGH NUTRITION

Like iridology, nutrition is a science still in its infancy, and there is much more to be learned about both. Yet, even in their present state of development, iridology and nutrition work hand in hand. Iris analysis reveals the organs, glands and tissues in need of nutrients, since all lesions in the acute, subacute, chronic or degenerative stage reveal nutrient deficiencies; and when we know the specific nutrients to provide for rebuilding particular types of tissue, we can design a nutritional program for each individual patient.

Mr. R.P., age 64, came to me with severe skin problems and allergies. Notice the photos on the following page of Mr. R.P. He had seen several doctors, but none were able to help. Years before, itchy, scaly spots appeared on top of his head and spread to the elbows and eventually covered his arms and legs. "I used a steel rasp to file the rough, scaly dead skin off," he reported. "I could pinch the rough, dead scales and not even feel it."

At least one doctor thought it was psoriasis, and another thought he had liver problems. Mr. R.P's. back and joints were

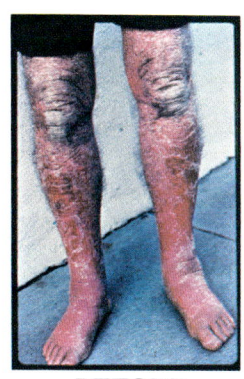 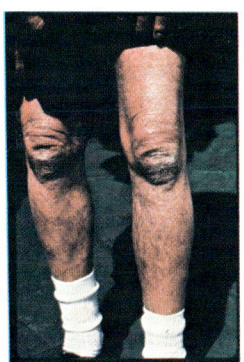 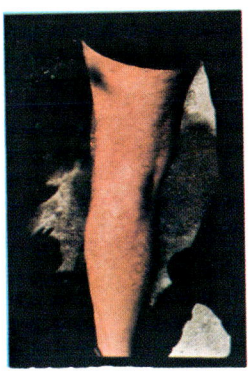

BEFORE　　　　　AFTER　　　　　AFTER

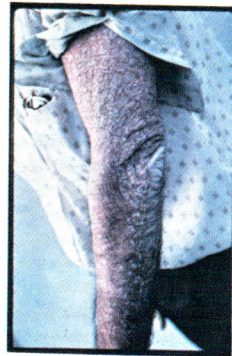 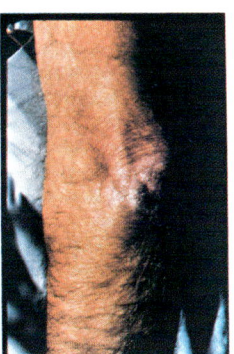

BEFORE　　　　　AFTER

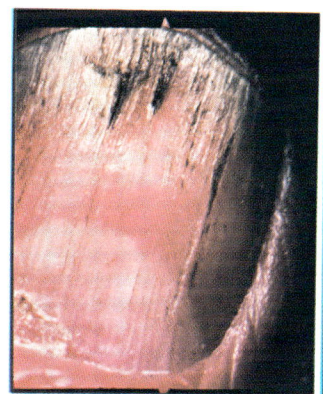 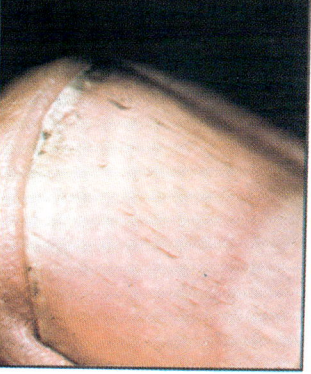

BEFORE　　　　　AFTER

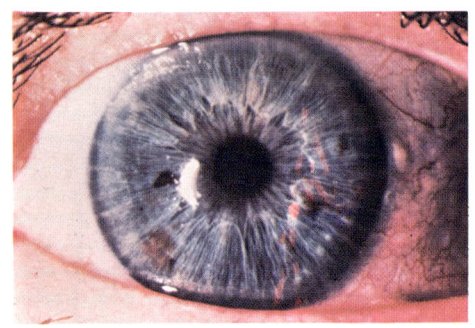

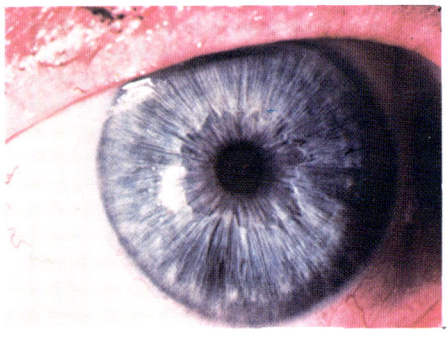

stiff and painful, "as though rheumatism was setting in," as he put it.

Iridology showed extreme acidity and catarrh, while the dark ring around the periphery of both irides showed skin elimination was poor. Both kidneys were underactive, the left one espoecially. His irides displayed an acid stomach, bronchial catarrh, poor leg circulation, inherent weaknesses in the bowel and bronchial areas, underactive liver, lymph gland congestion, nerve rings, inherent weaknesses in the pancreas and back area. The colon was pocketed with diverticula.

Mr. R.P. had depleted his body's reserves of silicon through excessively high stress mental work to the point of abuse of the nervous system. Unsuitable occupations, resentment and resistance appeared to be factors in depleting the nerves. When too much silicon is used up in the nervous system, we find the reserves in the skin, hair and nails can become depleted, making the skin vulnerable to disease.

He began to use my basic diet and was asked to avoid citrus, head lettuce, bread, wheat and oatmeal. I suggested he add sprouts (high in silicon) to his daily diet, digestive aids, bone marrow, diuretic herbs, vitamins A, C and E and protomorphogens, including a protomorphogen to stimulate drainage of the congested lymph glands.

Four months later, new skin began to appear without the rough scales. Nature works slowly, but she is sure in her ways. In about a year's time, R.P. looked and felt very well. His digestion was better; the nerves had calmed down; and he was at peace. Notice the healing lines in the irides pictures on page 54, corresponding to improvements in skin and nails shown in the photos.

Keep in mind that no diet can compensate for an extreme lifestyle, a lifestyle in which tissue is breaking down faster than it can be built up with foods. Unless a patient is willing to make appropriate changes and work toward health, no doctor or therapy can help.

7-DAY CHANGE

Mr. R.M., a 60-year-old insurance salesman, came to my office with raw, greenish, running ulcers on both ankles and feet, which were swollen and infected. One doctor had suggested amputation, since various treatments had failed to bring improvement. R.M. opposed this option, because leg problems ran in his family and because his grandfather had died of gangrene after a series of amputations (starting at the ankle), with later reinfections at each stump. The amputations had not solved the problems for his grandfather. R.M's. mother and one brother had died of colitis.

For the previous 7-1/2 years, R.M. had severe diarrhea with 7-to-8 bowel movements per day.

Iris analysis showed black in the bowel area, indicating extreme underactivity and heavy toxic settlements, with inherent weakness in kidneys and underactive adrenal glands. In the leg areas, a combination of poor circulation, enervation and toxic

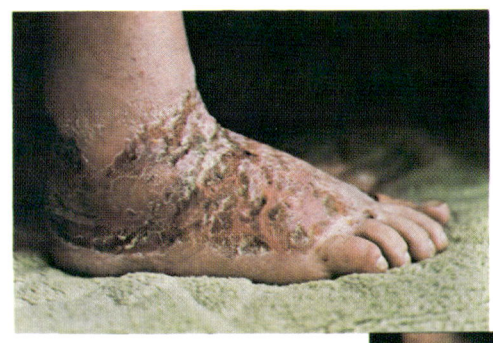
BEFORE

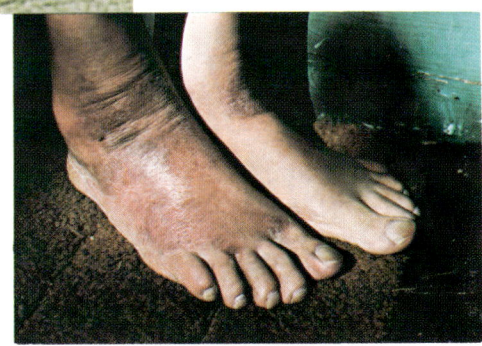
AFTER

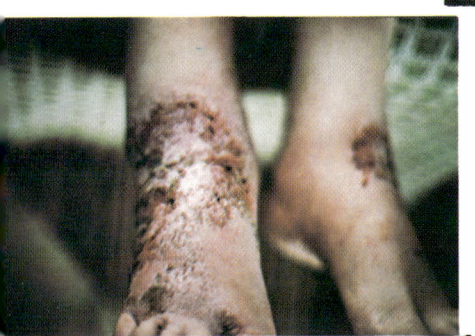
BEFORE

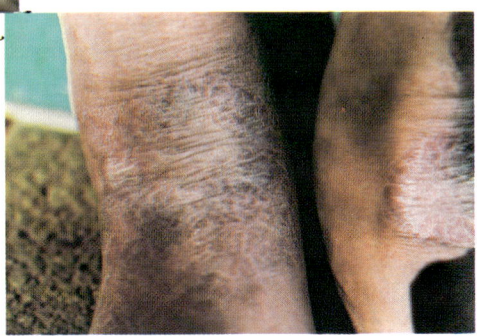
AFTER

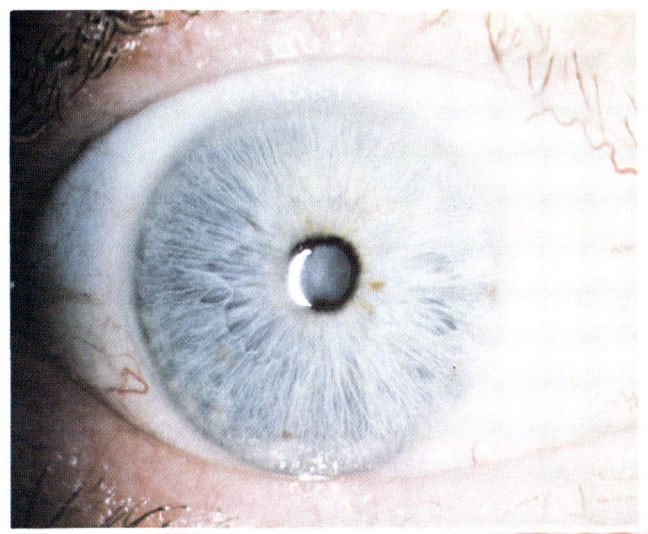

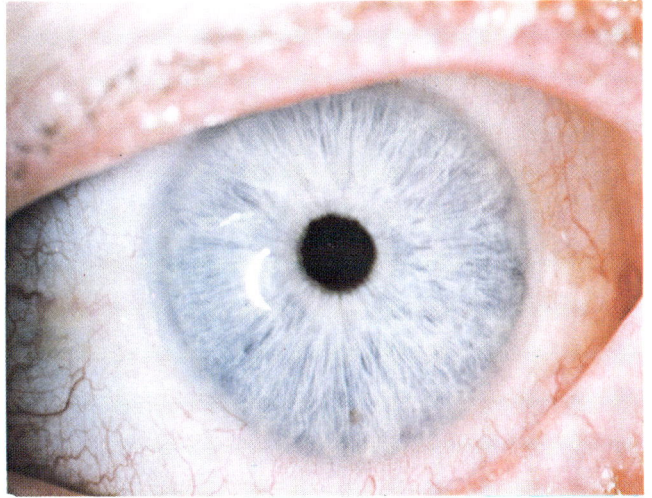

settlements accounted, in part, for the extreme problems he was having.

While helpful dietary changes were made, the most dramatic results were obtained by cleansing the bowel through my 7-day colema program. The colema is a cross between an enema and a colonic, and when it is administered for 7 days with the right bulk, supplements, etc., it is very efficient in removing toxic material from the bowel and the rest of the body.

In R.M's. case, I can say I have never seen healing take place so rapidly. It was dramatic. Apparently, the removal of the toxic material was the key to replacement of old tissue with new in his feet and ankles. Notice the constitutional strength in R.M's. irides, demonstrated by the fine weave of the iris fibers, like silk. This indicates potential for rapid healing. The 7-day change is shown in the previously shown photographs.

An extreme lack of silicon, sodium and calcium contributed to his problem, but the toxic bowel and underactive kidneys were also major factors.

When his wife drove to the Ranch to pick him up at the end of his 7-day program, he was able to wear shoes for the first time in several months. The swelling was greatly reduced.

At home, using my regular diet regimen and a few supplements, R.M. continued to improve. The diarrhea left and normal bowel movements returned. Two years later, R.M. appeared on television, and described what he had gone through. He said, "I am completely free of any leg or foot problems."

COMPUTERS IN IRIDOLOGY

Not only will computers provide us with micro-level information about the iris, but they will be able to correlate this information in new ways. Theoretically, it is possible to develop a computer program that will "think" wholistically, analyzing each organ's effects on all the others. For example, the computer might be able to tell us what effect upon the liver an 11% breakdown in pancreas tissue will have. It might also predict what the effects on the digestive system would be, and print out a list of foods to avoid.

At present, our computer has the capability of looking closely at the edges of a particular lesion and enhancing the data to tell us whether the lesion boundary is well-defined, broken up or faded out. That is, the computer and scanner serve as an extension of the human eye, seeing what we cannot.

In the upper right photograph, notice the iridology grid placed over the iris. Analysis of tissue function levels in the kidney has been done, quantified on the bar graph shown in the lower left quadrant of the picture. This can give us the percentages of tissue at each level of activity.

The bottom picture shows how the computer can enhance contrast in the iris, assigning easily distinguished colors in place of the white, gray, dark gray and black shades that reflexly reveal the levels of tissue activity we call acute, subacute, chronic and degenerative.

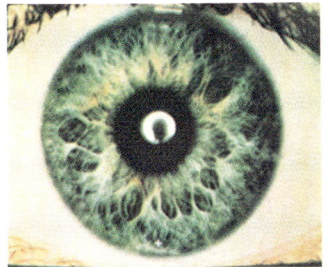

**COMPUTER IMAGE:
TRUE COLOR**

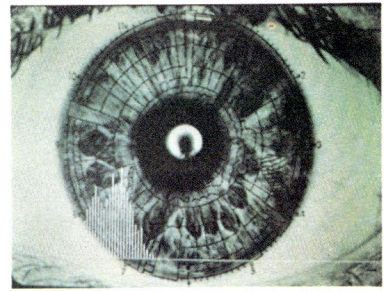

**TISSUE ACTIVITY
LEVELS: KIDNEY**

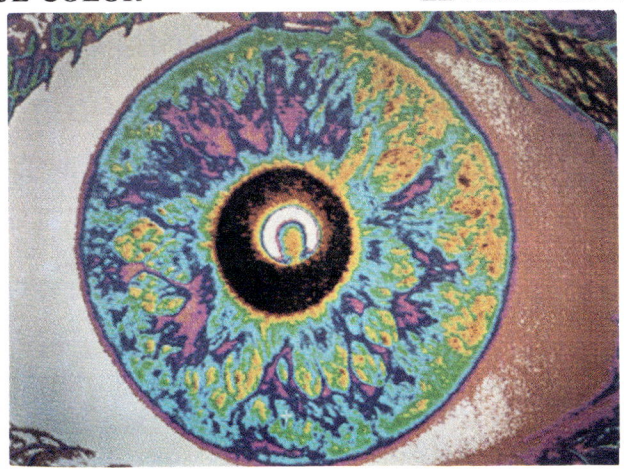

**COMPUTER IMAGE: PSEUDO COLOR
Pink (acute); Blue (subacute);
Green (chronic); Red (degenerative)**

NEW INSTRUMENTATION

Space-Age technology is introducing a new dimension in iridology, ushering in a level of precision, reliability and usefulness that will at last bring this fledgling science the recognition it deserves. I believe that the greatest advances in iridology are yet to come, and I believe the validity of iridology will be established beyond the shadow of a doubt in the next few years.

Notice in the iris picture at the top of the following page, the kidney lesion at about 6 o'clock. Obviously, we have an underactivity here, a clear indication that the kidney is unable to function normally. Now this is sufficient to tell us that we need to change the diet to take care of this condition, but we would like to know more, and we can know more.

I use a precision camera with a special lens to take color slides of most of the irides I analyze, but I also still look at peoples' eyes with a four-power magnifying glass and a penlight, when they come for a checkup. The problem with both direct and photographic examination is the subjectivity involved. One iridologist might say a certain lesion is chronic (dark gray). Another might say it is degenerative (black). Who is right? One iridologist could say the healing lines are unchanged in a lesion, while another could say there are more than before. Again, who is right?

We have solved this problem. By hooking up a computer with a video scanner, we can have the computer analyze the irides with a precision, accuracy, consistency and repeatability never before possible. Our computer is not limited to evaluating lesions according to the four color gradations of white, gray, dark gray and black. It can easily distinguish between ten shades, a hundred shades or a thousand shades—as many as we want. This technology is being refined right now so we will have full use of it soon.

With computer-interpreted video scans, we can take an iris photo like the one shown on the following page and get a

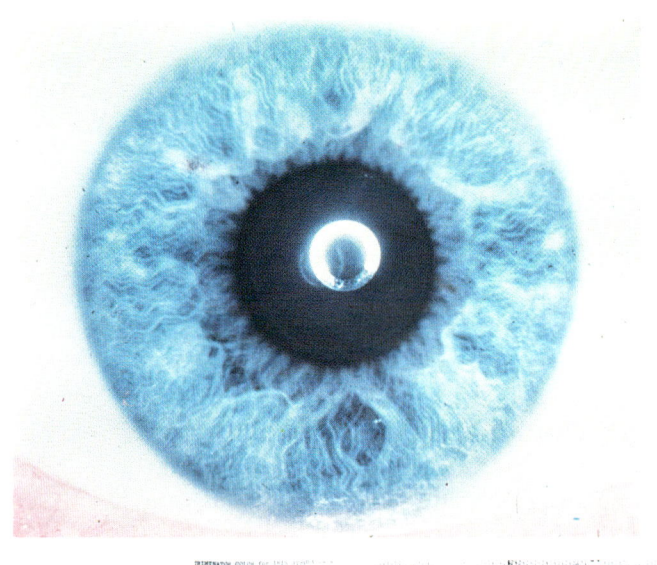

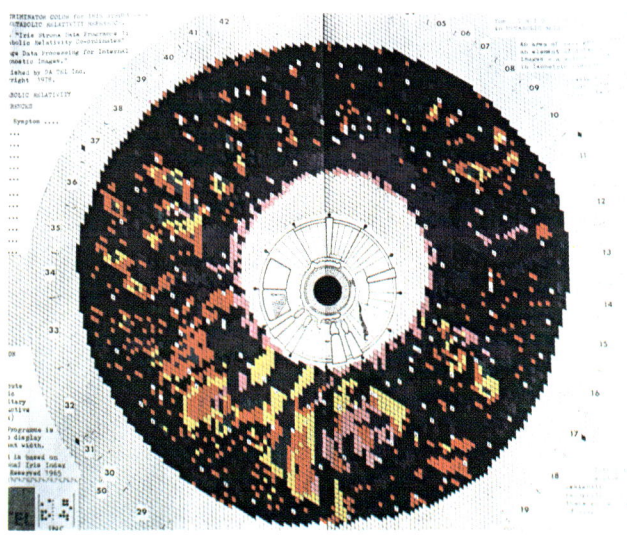

readout that tells the percentage of healing lines in that kidney lesion. We can store this information in computer memory, take another photo two weeks later, and find out whether that kidney is improving or declining. We can do the same thing in six months, a year or two years.

We may be able to establish precise reflex relationships among the organs, identifying which ones are triggering reflex conditions in others. Those with the darkest lesions will be the ones influencing those not quite as dark.

It will not be long before we can get the computer to analyze a person's irides and give us a readout on exactly what vitamins and minerals are needed, along with a list of foods to take care of those deficiencies. As the patient goes on his or her new diet, the computer will monitor progress.

In the computer color-coded iris at the bottom of the previous page, we see the computer has translated the original shades of the iris shown in the top photo to allow an easier identification of shades. The spectrum of white to black shading has been translated into eight colors: white, blue, yellow, red, green, violet, magenta and black. I can easily distinguish between yellow and red, but I would have great difficulty telling the difference between two shades of medium gray.

I believe the computer is going to help us understand much more about the brain area represented in the iris from 11 to 1 o'clock. This is perhaps the one area of the iris that we know least about.

The three pictures at the top of the next page are sonaradiology grids displaying isometric patterns developed by computer.

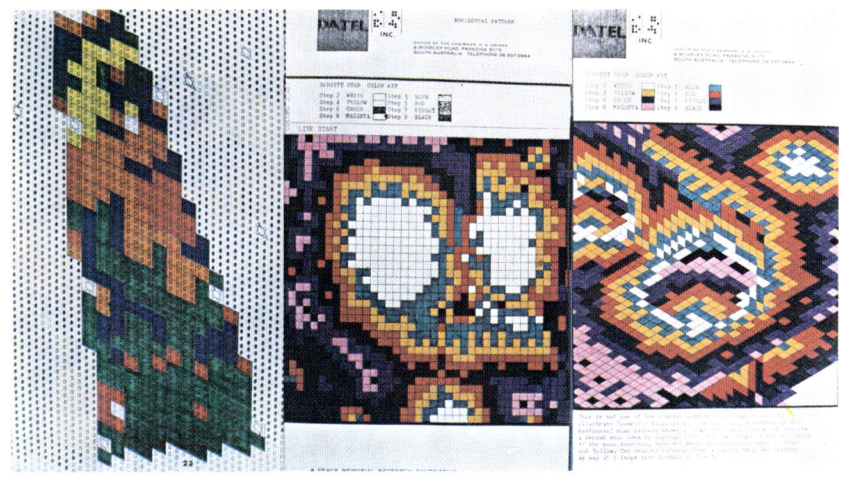

WILL PROVE IT

The top photo on the following page is the famous picture of the planet Earth taken during one of the Apollo missions. From a distance, we see atmosphere patterns, surface patterns and they mean very little until we get "down to earth" and encounter seas, continents, polar ice caps, tropical zones, a variety of climates, types of people, animal life, vegetation and geophysical phenomena. The iris is a similar "world of its own," with a great deal of meaning to its structure and organization, but it only reveals this information to those who take the time to study it.

The two middle pictures, a planetary surface and a moon shot, were taken from NASA space vehicles. The instrumentation aboard these vehicles is amazing in terms of information-gathering capability. With a video scanner hooked up to a computer, the surface topography can be accurately charted—the depths of craters, the heights of peaks, the configuration of plains, mountains, valleys, fissures and all the various landscape features. This information is stored in a computer and can be reproduced at will for scientists to

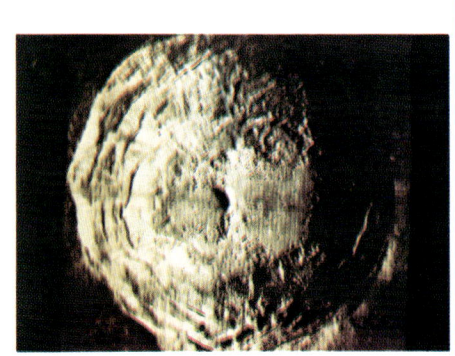

examine. This space-age technology can also be applied to the iris to prove iridology—and to extend its present boundaries and applications.

On the photo page following, we see my latest Iriscope 113CW camera. Since beginning to use photography, I have gone through 112 cameras, designing improved features each time. The camera is mounted on a frame to stabilize the head while photos are taken of the iris, illuminated by a fiber optics light source. These are the basic tools of today's iridologist. The white ring or crescent moon appearing on or near the iris photos presented in previous illustrations is a reflection of the fiber optics light source.

The great advantage of photography, of course, is that it gives the iridologist and the patient a permanent record of iris changes. Photographs taken at intervals of months or years show whether progress is being made, whether tissue in the body is being repaired. Every doctor should have a reliable means of checking his work. A patient may say, "I feel great," and mean it, but there may well be another year's work before the actual tissue changes have taken place.

I believe there is much more in the eye that we will ever know. In *System of Ophthalmology* by Stewart, Duke and Elder (Vol. II), the authors state, "The network of nerves (in the iris) is extraordinarily rich, so much so that...every stromal cell and chromatophore receives its own nerve supply." These nerves are constantly relaying information from the autonomic nervous system to the irides concerning the state of every part of the body. At present, our analysis of the iris is based on macro-events, phenomena large enough to be visible to the naked eye, but a scanner can "look at" units as small as one ten-thousandths of an inch. When we begin studying micro-evens in the iris, I believe it will be like exploring a whole new world.

**If you are interested in
the 113CW Jensen
Iris Camera System, write for a free copy
of our new camera brochure.**

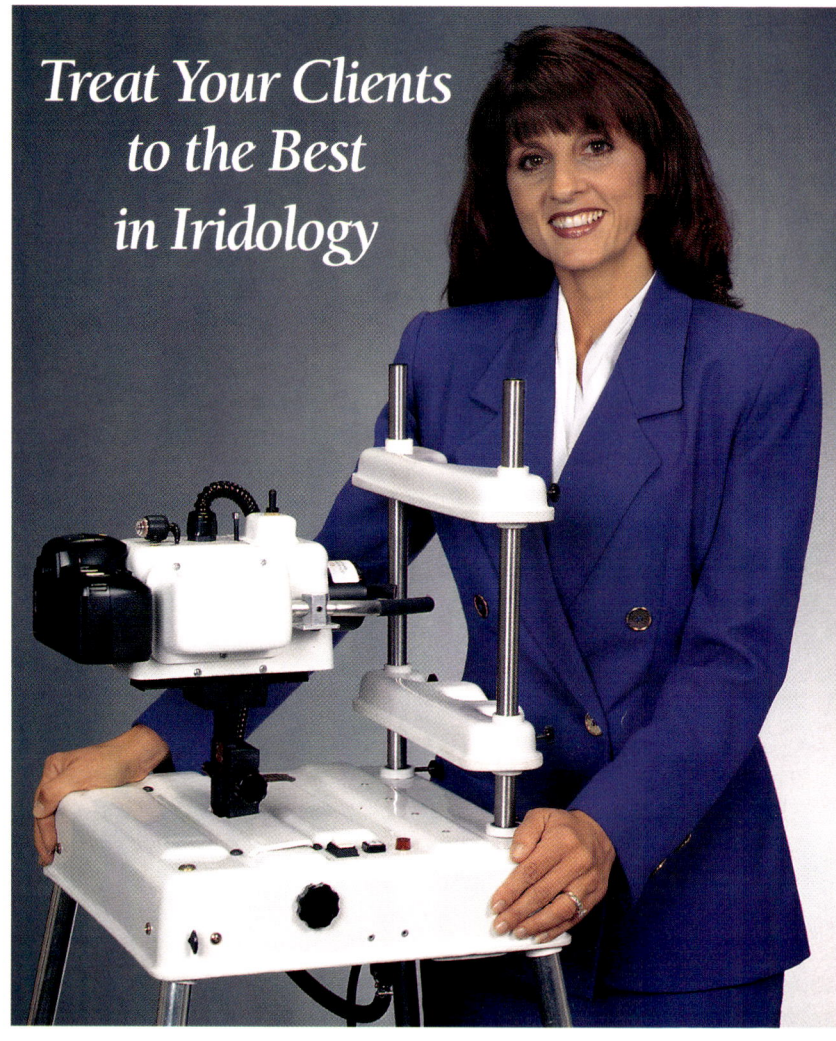

Develop Your Skills, Build Your Practice and Help Others with the Jensen Iridology System

Model 113CW Features
- Patented fiber-optic lighting system filters out all harmful ultraviolet radiation
- Includes everything you need to take gorgeous photos of the iris
- Rugged padded carrying cases included
- Parts and labor guaranteed for one year

*Easy to Use — Takes Superb Photographs
Designed and Built to Last for Years*